G000054306

Transparency in Government Operations

George Kopits and Jon Craig

INTERNATIONAL MONETARY FUND

Washington DC

January 1998

Cataloging-in-Publication Data

Kopits, George.
    Transparency in government operations / George Kopits and Jon Craig.

      p.   cm.—(Occasional paper, ISSN 0251-6365 ; 158)

"February 1998."
Includes bibliographical references.

ISBN 1-55775-697-X

    1. Finance, Public—Accounting. 2. Fiscal policy. I. Craig, J.D. (Jon D.) II. International Monetary Fund. III. Title. IV. Series: Occasional paper (International Monetary Fund) ; no. 158.
HJ9733.K66   1998

336.3—dc21   97-51353
                                                                CIP

Price: US$18.00
(US$15.00 to full-time faculty members and
students at universities and colleges)

Please send orders to:
International Monetary Fund, Publication Services
700 19th Street, N.W., Washington, D.C. 20431, U.S.A.
Tel.: (202) 623-7430   Telefax: (202) 623-7201
E-mail: publications@imf.org
Internet: http://www.imf.org

recycled paper

Contents

The following symbols have been used throughout this paper:

. . . to indicate that data are not available;

— to indicate that the figure is zero or less than half the final digit shown, or that the item does not exist;

– between years or months (e.g., 1994–95 or January–June) to indicate the years or months covered, including the beginning and ending years or months;

/ between years (e.g., 1994/95) to indicate a crop or fiscal (financial) year.

"Billion" means a thousand million.

Minor discrepancies between constituent figures and totals are due to rounding.

The term "country," as used in this paper, does not in all cases refer to a territorial entity that is a state as understood by international law and practice; the term also covers some territorial entities that are not states, but for which statistical data are maintained and provided internationally on a separate and independent basis.

Preface

This paper was prepared by George Kopits, Assistant Director, and Jon Craig, Senior Economist, Fiscal Affairs Department. They wish to acknowledge contributions by Hugh Young and other members of the department's Fiscal Analysis Division. Also, many colleagues in different departments reviewed the factual accuracy and reasoning at various stages from inception to completion. In particular, the paper has benefited from comments and encouragement from Stanley Fischer, Peter Heller, Flemming Larsen, Thomas McLoughlin, A. Premchand, Vito Tanzi, and Teresa Ter-Minassian. The authors are indebted to Diana Ellyn and Beulah David for secretarial assistance, to Diane Cross for editorial support, to Elisa Diehl of the External Relations Department for editing the final version and coordinating production, and to Alicia Etchebarne-Bourdin for composition.

An earlier draft of the paper was discussed by the Executive Board in October 1997. The present version incorporates the suggestions received on that occasion. However, the opinions expressed are those of the authors and do not necessarily reflect the views of the Executive Directors, the management, or the staff of the International Monetary Fund.

I Introduction

Transparency in government operations is widely regarded as an important precondition for macroeconomic fiscal sustainability, good governance, and overall fiscal rectitude. Notably, the Interim Committee, at its April and September 1996 meetings, stressed the need for greater fiscal transparency. Specifically, in the Declaration on Partnership for Sustainable Global Growth, the Committee stated that "it is essential to enhance the transparency of fiscal policy by persevering with efforts to reduce off-budget transactions and quasi-fiscal deficits" (International Monetary Fund, 1996c, p. xii). Prompted by these concerns, this paper represents a first attempt to address many of the aspects of transparency in government operations. It provides an overview of major issues in fiscal transparency and examines the IMF's role in promoting transparency in government operations. It is, however, not to be viewed as a comprehensive compendium of transparent practices.

Conceptual Setting

Fiscal transparency is defined in this paper as openness toward the public at large about government structure and functions, fiscal policy intentions, public sector accounts, and projections. It involves ready access to reliable, comprehensive, timely, understandable, and internationally comparable information on government activities—whether undertaken inside or outside the government sector—so that the electorate and financial markets can accurately assess the government's financial position and the true costs and benefits of government activities, including their present and future economic and social implications.

Transparency in government operations has several dimensions. First, at an aggregate level, transparency requires the provision of reliable information on the government's fiscal policy intentions and forecasts. Second, detailed data and information are required on government operations, including the publication of comprehensive budget documents that contain properly classified accounts for the general government and estimates of quasi-fiscal activities conducted outside the government. The third dimension consists of mainly behavioral aspects, including clearly established conflict-of-interest rules for elected and appointed officials, freedom-of-information requirements, a transparent regulatory framework, open public procurement and employment practices, a code of conduct for tax officials, and published performance audits. In all three dimensions, fiscal transparency is closely associated with the successful implementation of good governance.[1] While this paper provides an overview of measures to strengthen behavioral aspects, it chiefly focuses on the first two dimensions of fiscal transparency, which are generally more amenable to IMF surveillance (Section III). In particular, it seeks to identify specific practices (e.g., transparency in fiscal statistics and targets as well as budget and tax collection procedures) that enhance good governance through greater visibility to the public.

From a practical standpoint, it is necessary to distinguish between deliberate secrecy, or misreporting, and a technical inability to provide certain information (e.g., owing to inadequate data collection systems). The latter is usually attributable to the slow pace of technical or administrative development, which can be corrected through training and institution building, supported by technical assistance. A deliberate lack of fiscal transparency is often attributable to a government's attempt to escape public scrutiny of its behavior[2]—especially in the run-up to elections—to avoid or postpone possible adverse reaction from the electorate and from financial markets, on which it depends for political support and deficit financing, respectively.

Pressures to engage in nontransparent practices are likely to mount during periods of fiscal stress. Rather than take unpopular corrective action, gov-

---

[1]The linkage between fiscal transparency and good governance is discussed, for example, in World Bank (1994).

[2]Public choice theory emphasizes the incentive of governments to understate the actual costs and overstate the benefits associated with specific policy decisions, exploiting the fiscal illusion of voters. See, for example, the discussion in Buchanan and Wagner (1976) and an early treatment in Puviani (1903).

ernments may resort to such practices when facing difficulties in meeting near-term budget targets.[3] Such budget targets may be either self-imposed or pursuant to an outside commitment—including in the context of an IMF-supported program. A current illustration is provided by the creative accounting practices adopted in some member countries of the European Union (EU) to meet the fiscal criteria specified under the Maastricht Treaty.[4]

Arguments For and Against Fiscal Transparency

Fiscal transparency, in each of its three dimensions, is a necessary condition for sound economic policy. Timely publication of a clearly presented budget document makes it easier for the market to evaluate the government's intentions and allows the market itself to impose a constructive discipline on the government. Transparency increases the political risk of unsustainable policies, whereas the lack thereof means that fiscal profligacy can go undetected longer than it otherwise would. Similarly, a transparent public financial accounting system makes it possible for the market to determine what the government has actually done and to compare budgeted and actual financial operations. Fiscal transparency—including, for example, open procurement practices—not only facilitates the achievement of the basic macroeconomic policy objectives, but also increases the productivity of public expenditure. More generally, transparency, by increasing the trust that the population reposes in the government, has a salutary effect on society and the economy. There are thus strong a priori reasons for arguing that transparency improves the performance of the economy.

It may, however, be difficult to prove that fiscal transparency always leads to better policy settings that are, in turn, translated into improved fiscal and economic outcomes. The difficulty stems partly from the fact that transparent practices are only one influence on the overall outcome and partly from the problems encountered in specifying the counterfactual experience.

In general, countries characterized by a relatively high degree of fiscal transparency have exhibited greater fiscal discipline and, in many instances, have been able to achieve a more robust economic performance than other broadly comparable—in terms of resource endowment and cultural characteristics—countries with less transparent practices within the same region.[5] There are countries where secrecy in government operations and a lack of discipline contributed to a disastrous economic performance, despite an ample resource endowment.[6] In a broader context, the recent crisis in Southeast and East Asia illustrates that transparency in the financial sector—including the extent of government-directed or -guaranteed lending—is a prerequisite for sustained growth. Also, cross-country studies suggest a positive relationship between broadly defined transparent budget practices and fiscal discipline.[7] Although evidence points to a positive linkage between fiscal transparency and performance, corroboration of the relationship would require a more systematic documentation of country practices.

Nontransparent fiscal practices tend to be destabilizing, to create allocative distortions, and to exacerbate inequities. These adverse repercussions may not be apparent in the near term,[8] but may surface later in the form of a severe financial crisis, requiring much costlier remedial action. For instance, nontransparent tax concessions, quasi-fiscal subsidies, and off-budget spending all contribute to fiscal imbalances. The destabilizing consequences of an accumulation of payment arrears and of unfunded contingent liabilities are usually felt with longer lags. More immediately, governments that do not disclose

---

[3]According to Goodhart's law—named after Professor Charles Goodhart's observation about targeting monetary aggregates—a statistical indicator ceases to be reliable once it is declared an official target for policy purposes.

[4]Although creative accounting practices associated with these fiscal criteria have been given considerable attention in the media, it is particularly their future implications—including the additional measures needed to compensate for the insufficient fiscal adjustment at the outset—that lack transparency. The broader issue is that creative accounting damages the credibility of the fiscal criteria, and thus their effectiveness, when the countries engaging in such practices are seen as not adhering to the criteria.

[5]The country experiences presented in Appendix IV provide some support for this view. Indeed, Botswana, Chile, Denmark, and New Zealand, which display considerable fiscal transparency and discipline, have experienced macroeconomic stability and strong growth in recent years. Both Hungary and Jordan, despite major handicaps relative to other countries in their respective regions (i.e., high indebtedness and a lack of a significant resource endowment), have seen an improvement in economic performance while implementing fiscal adjustment in an increasingly transparent context.

[6]The former members of the Council for Mutual Economic Assistance (CMEA) operated, under socialist central planning, with opaque budget documents and budget process, a large number of nonparametric turnover taxes and subsidies, and a proliferation of fiscal and quasi-fiscal activities through branch ministries and the state-owned enterprise and banking sectors. See International Monetary Fund and others (1991).

[7]See Wagner (1976) for the United States, von Hagen and Harden (1994) for EU member countries, and Alesina and others (1995) for Latin America.

[8]Although fiscal transparency cannot guarantee consensus, there have been episodes (including recent ones) where a failure to prepare the population, through adequate and candid explanation, for the removal of a critical subsidy or of a labor market regulation has led to major unrest and jeopardized the improved economic performance sought by those measures.

sufficient information to financial markets are likely to incur an increased risk premium over time. All taxes and subsidies, as well as economic regulations, alter relative prices and factor returns and cause distortions in resource allocation. In addition, however, when they are not transparent, the harmful impact of these practices, including the benefits they may provide to influential interest groups at the expense of poorer and less vocal groups, is hidden from public view and debate.

Fiscal transparency can also impose costs. Obviously, up-front costs are incurred in creating the technical capacity and institutions to establish a centralized information system, develop reliable forecasting tools, implement appropriate accounting techniques, and simplify regulatory practices or make their cost visible. Moreover, there are recurrent, albeit often declining, costs in maintaining these practices and disseminating the generated information. The costs of transforming a culture of secrecy into one of transparency may be at least equally large.

Whereas institutional arrangements and accounting practices in the public sector must always be transparent to reap the known benefits, the timing of public disclosure as to the formulation of government decisions may require some judgment. In some cases, broad policy goals, including the fiscal targets and the measures to achieve them, are announced as soon as they are decided; following the announcement, a debate may ensue, and the initial targets and measures may be altered in the light of that debate. However, alternative approaches may work equally well. For example, some political leaders may choose to air policy targets and intentions informally in an attempt to test public opinion and generate the necessary consensus to carry out, or modify, those policy intentions. In any event, deliberations within each branch of government on specific features and timing of the measures being considered may have to be closed to the public to avoid undue influence from more powerful and active lobby groups.[9]

Generally speaking, once the decision is reached on a given measure, it should be publicly announced unless it is a component of a broader policy package. In that event, a delay may be justified until the entire package is ready to be unveiled, to preserve the integrity of the package. For example, a real wage cut for civil servants in the context of the draft budget that is announced before agreement is reached with the relevant labor representatives may undermine the government's position at the negotiating table and unravel the coherence of the budget.[10]

Transparency entails risks when the resulting behavior of some groups may be inimical to the general welfare or may erode the effectiveness of a specific policy instrument. For example, in conducting monetary policy, the authorities refrain from revealing their intentions about a future exchange rate or interest rate action to maximize its effectiveness and minimize windfall gains to certain economic agents.[11] In the fiscal area, premature announcement of the introduction of a subsidy or tax incentive may also weaken its intended effect and result in a windfall gain for some agents and an unnecessary budgetary cost. Announcement of, say, an investment tax credit prior to its effective date may induce enterprises to postpone investment expenditures they would have undertaken without the tax credit. Symmetrically, announcing the repeal of an existing tax credit before the effective date may induce an acceleration of capital formation that would take place anyway. Likewise, announcement of future tariff cuts (increases) may induce a postponement (an acceleration) of imports prior to the effective date of the policy action.[12] The foregoing considerations are, to an extent, comparable to basic principles of transparency, namely, simultaneous release of, and equal access to, statistical information to avoid unfair rent seeking. These principles do not, of course, preclude administrative practices that restrict prerelease access to sensitive information, for a short time, to key government officials.[13]

In general, provision for contingencies should be made explicit in policy statements and budget documents. However, there are situations where for tactical reasons governments may choose to adopt implicitly a somewhat conservative set of underlying macroeconomic assumptions or fiscal parameters in formulating and submitting a draft budget so as to re-

---

[9]In the United States, for example, according to Reese (1979), it was observed that since 1971, when legislative markup sessions became open to the public, congressmen have relied increasingly on political aides and have been exposed to greater pressures from special interest groups, whereas previously they resorted to a largely apolitical technical staff and were somewhat protected from such pressures.

---

[10]Further, it could be argued that the premature disclosure of information about the likely adverse effects of pending discretionary measures on certain groups may be counterproductive—risking a policy reversal once the information becomes available—especially where the more general benefits of the measures may not be understood or quantifiable.

[11]On the reaction of financial markets to secrecy in monetary policy, see Tabellini (1987).

[12]By the same token, tax preferences intended to promote a given activity, when granted retroactively—say, to the beginning of the fiscal year—confer a windfall gain on economic agents who would have engaged in it without the preferences. Retroactive elimination of the tax preference is tantamount to imposing a tax and may be seen as unfair to those who had counted on the preference when taking their decisions.

[13]These practices are explicitly recognized under the IMF's Special Data Dissemination Standard (SDDS).

duce the downside risk of a subsequent weakening of the fiscal stance by the legislature. Along similar lines, in some countries, the authorities may be reluctant to reveal the accumulation of fiscal surpluses—stemming, for example, from an unexpected rise in the world price of a key export commodity or from a windfall gain from privatization—for fear of pressure to ease the fiscal policy stance.[14] The merits of other, time-inconsistent, arguments for secrecy or ambiguity—beneficial to elected officials[15]—cannot be viewed as a prescription for best practice.

In summary, the case for fiscal transparency rests on the fundamental principles of public finance: stability, efficiency, and fairness. Overall, fiscal transparency tends to be associated with fiscal discipline and enhances good governance, thus contributing to improved economic performance. Because transparency leads to government accountability—whereas, conversely, statutory accountability requirements can bring about transparent practices—and credibility, the beneficial effects are reflected in lower risk premiums in financial markets and stronger support of government policies by a well-informed electorate.[16] Nonetheless, the arguments in favor of transparency are subject to certain caveats; under certain well-defined circumstances and for a limited time, access to sensitive budget data or information on specific policy measures that may confer unfair benefits on some groups may have to be restricted to a few key government officials.

---

[14]The less-than-full public disclosure of large foreign exchange reserve holdings or the earmarking of externally generated fiscal surpluses to hidden off-budget accounts, for prudential reasons, has been a hallmark of some countries in Southeast Asia and the Middle East.

[15]See Alesina and Cukierman (1990) for examples of institutional arrangements and practices that maximize politicians' chances of being reelected while concealing their true ideological preferences: relying on legislative subcommittees and task forces, avoiding roll-call voting, and secretly influencing monetary authorities and then using them as scapegoats.

[16]The central role of the government budget in this process has been acknowledged, for example, in the United States (President's Commission on Budget Concepts, 1967): the budget should provide "the public with information ... essential for private business, labor, agriculture, and other groups, and for an informed assessment by citizens of governmental stewardship of the public's money and resources" (p. 2). And, in turn, the public "must be able to participate intelligently in the big decisions that come to focus there: the overall size of government; the relative emphasis on different government programs and activities intended to benefit the Nation; the efficiency and effectiveness of major government programs in the light of their intended purposes; the need for tax increases or the opportunities for tax cuts; and fiscal policies designed to promote national prosperity" (p. 11).

II   Issues in Fiscal Transparency

This section reviews the major facets of fiscal transparency in three overlapping and interrelated areas.[17] The first encompasses transparency in government institutions and behavior. To secure support for fiscal policy and its implementation, the authorities must inform the public about the overall structure of government, as reflected in the relations between the public sector and private agents and in the interactions within the public sector. These include openness in the budget process, tax policy statutes and administration, the government's financing operations, and the nature and costs of the regulatory framework. The second area consists of transparency in public accounts—that is, the measurement of government transactions, ownership, and obligations—required for sound fiscal policy-making. For this purpose, it is necessary to focus on the coverage, recording basis, valuation, recognition, and classification of relevant flows and stocks. The third area deals with the transparency of summary indicators used to assess fiscal policy stance and sustainability as well as of projections of fiscal aggregates—all dependent on the quality and transparency of public accounts.

Institutional Framework

A basic requirement for transparency in the *overall structure and functions* of government is a clear demarcation of the boundaries between the public and private sectors (Box 1). Apart from some activities (e.g., education, health care, and public utilities) where both sectors may operate concurrently, in many countries, the government is solely responsible for public administration, internal safety, defense, foreign relations, and macroeconomic policy. As part of the delineation of areas of competence, it is essential to limit private rent seeking by officials in the public domain through enforcement of conflict-of-interest legislation. Meanwhile, freedom-of-information legislation helps ensure government transparency and accountability by giving citizens access to public documents and assigning to government the burden of justifying nondisclosure.

Within the public sector, it is necessary to maintain transparency in the relations between the government and the state-owned enterprise sector. Although there are sound reasons for limiting the extent to which this sector is engaged in activities more legitimately carried out by the government, where such practices nevertheless occur, it is important that they be well documented in publicly available reports. Similarly, in spite of the general trend toward managing and operating state-owned enterprises along commercial lines, many enterprises still incur losses from nontransparent quasi-fiscal activities (e.g., in providing social benefits). Equally, the cost of quasi-fiscal activities conducted by public or private financial institutions—through multiple exchange rates, preferential credits, and guarantees—is frequently not made explicit or even calculated. Regardless of the actual budgetary treatment of quasi-fiscal activities,[18] information should be provided—preferably in annual budget documents—on the associated cost (or gain). Conversely, documentation should be made available when government ministries perform activities that would normally be performed in the state-owned enterprise sector.

A related issue of major concern is the provision of adequate information on the fiscal costs and the terms of assistance or of restructuring of public (or, in some cases, private) financial institutions and nonfinancial enterprises.[19] Similarly, privatization of such entities must be conducted with as much openness as permitted by sound marketing considerations.

Responsibility for expenditures on basic public services and functions needs to be clearly divided

---

[17]For a more detailed discussion of these issues, see Appendices I through III.

[18]Namely, regardless of whether enterprises are compensated or not with explicit transfers from the budget for the cost of quasi-fiscal activities.

[19]For a survey of bank rescue operations, see Alexander and others (1997).

Box 1. Summary of Good Practices in Institutional Transparency

Overall structure and functions

Clear demarcation of functions between public and private sectors.

Delineation of the boundaries of the operations of state-owned nonfinancial enterprises and financial institutions from those of the general government; and provision of information on the costs of quasi-fiscal activities performed by such enterprises and institutions, as well as any financial rescue operations funded by the government.

Clear assignment of responsibilities and resources among national and subnational levels of government (limiting the scope for case-by-case negotiation).

Clear statement of the rationale for, and extent of, extrabudgetary fund operations.

Establishment of an independent review agency with wide investigative authority over government operations.

Budget process

Detailed public explanation of fiscal targets and priorities in the draft budget.

Open legislative debate and authorization.

Transparent execution and control (including procurement, contracting, and employment).

Public disclosure of results of performance and financial audits.

Tax treatment

Explicit statutory basis (instead of discretionary tax concessions or negotiated tax liabilities).

Clear administrative procedures, information requirements, taxpayers' rights and obligations, and tax officials' code of conduct.

Estimates of tax expenditure budget.

Financing operations

Disclosure of terms (interest yield and maturity) and sources of government deficit financing.

Specification of policy criteria as well as terms and conditions of government lending decisions.

Regulation

Open legislative and administrative process (e.g., hearings, approval).

Clear and simple statutes and implementation.

Estimates of regulatory costs.

---

between national and various subnational levels of government. Accordingly, the revenue base of each level of government should be defined unambiguously, possibly accompanied by formula-based arrangements for revenue sharing and intergovernmental transfers, thus limiting the room for ad hoc bargaining among jurisdictions.[20]

In principle, extrabudgetary operations can be efficient for pursuing certain tasks for which the spending obligation transcends the annual budget appropriation process.[21] Cases in point are social insurance and commodity stabilization funds. By contrast, in a number of countries, extrabudgetary funds—for instance, for military spending—have been created mainly to avoid legislative scrutiny. More often, funds originally established for valid reasons have become highly dysfunctional. For example, in some countries, easy access to old-age and disability pension funds is used nontransparently to alleviate unemployment. In

other countries, reserves accumulated in commodity stabilization funds—or, in general, reserve funds established from the sale of nonrenewable resources—have been diverted to finance consumer subsidies or prestige projects. Whatever the actual practices adopted, an important task facing governments is to ensure that adequate and timely information is provided on such activities. This should be done in a format that permits easy consolidation with that provided on other public sector activities.

A potentially important instrument for ensuring transparency in government operations is an independent review agency responsible for conducting performance audits and studies on selected fiscal issues. To be effective, such an agency must be accountable to the legislature and the public at large and must be endowed with wide investigative and reporting authority over government operations.

The tasks involved at each stage of the *budget process* are usually specified in some detail in the budget framework law or, less frequently, are based on past conventions and rulings. The draft budget—preferably incorporating broad fiscal targets and strategy in a multiyear context—should be disclosed in sufficient detail to the public, although the timing of the disclosure may need to be carefully controlled to ensure its coherence (Section I). The subsequent leg-

---

[20]Increasingly, in a number of countries, authorities at different levels of government are engaged in an open dialogue to set fiscal targets, delineate responsibilities, and prevent fiscal off-loading from one jurisdiction to another.

[21]Prompted largely by the need to prepare some government agencies for privatization, a recent practice of some EU member countries has been to move off-budget agencies that derive most of their revenue from user fees.

islative debate and approval should normally be open and the outcome published. At the execution stage, the government should periodically inform both the public and the legislature about the budgetary outcome and how it compares with the objectives. A further test of transparency in budget execution and control involves open public procurement, contracting, and employment practices. Finally, adequate information is necessary for conducting both financial and performance audits, and the results of such audits, including recommendations for and implementation of corrective steps, should be made public.

Transparency in *tax treatment* entails a well-defined statutory basis, as well as clear and simple administration—assisted by dissemination of all the necessary information, including filing instructions. Discretionary tax relief provided to particular individuals or enterprises or case-by-case negotiation of tax liabilities between tax officials and taxpayers, although unavoidable in some circumstances, impairs the transparency and credibility of the tax system. For greater transparency in tax administration, many countries have adopted statutes on taxpayers' rights and obligations, as well as rules of conduct for tax officials. As a justified departure from transparency (Section I), the announcement of changes in tax incentives should be timed to avoid eroding their cost-effectiveness.

Tax preferences can be viewed as tantamount to budgetary outlays benefiting certain households, enterprises, sectors, or activities. Estimates of tax expenditures—that is, revenue forgone because of tax preferences—are an important input for the debate of the annual draft budget or tax reform. Similarly, incidence studies can provide useful information about the distributional implications of the tax subsidy system. Although, admittedly, only some advanced economies have the technical capacity to prepare and publish such estimates on a regular basis, even approximate estimates of tax expenditures can facilitate the evaluation of the cost of tax preferences, including alternative proposals.

Transparency in government *financing operations* has been enhanced by financial deregulation. An increasing number of countries are relying on open, market-based financing (often from nonbank sources) of deficits while confirming the independence of the central bank and other public financial institutions. Such arrangements require provision of adequate data to market participants on such matters as timing of tenders, security issues, coupons offered, prices (and effective interest rate yields), and bids and offers accepted. Moreover, governments wishing to access international and domestic financial markets must furnish rating agencies, underwriters, and supervisory agencies with considerable data on the magnitude, terms (interest yield and matu-

rity), and holders of the public debt and on the government's debt-service capacity (often with a statement on its debt-management strategy). Of course, transparency in debt operations assumes even greater importance in a regulated market because the distortions introduced by constraints, such as required asset ratios for government security holdings, understate the true cost of financing the budget deficit at the expense of other lenders (which may include other components of general government, such as public pension funds). Transparency in government lending (directly or through financial institutions) entails adopting clearly specified policy criteria for loans made, including risk assessment, as well as releasing information on the terms and conditions of the loans.

Notwithstanding the justification for *regulation* in a number of areas (mainly public health, consumer safety, environmental protection, labor protection, and competition policy), a lack of clarity in the regulatory framework can lead to governance problems. Also, regulation is sometimes used as a nontransparent substitute for budget transfers or taxes. Unlike public services financed from the budget, the costs of compliance, whether borne directly by the regulated entities or indirectly by the rest of the economy, are not visible. The need to quantify regulatory costs is underscored by the temptation to substitute regulation for budgetary spending when governments attempt to compensate for pressures to cut government expenditures. In general, however, the movement toward deregulation in commodity, labor, and financial markets has contributed to greater transparency in government operations in this area.

Public Accounts

In principle, the general government is universally regarded as providing the most comprehensive coverage of the noncommercial public sector, consisting of the budget as well as social security and other extrabudgetary accounts, consolidated across all levels of government (Box 2).[22] However, even the concept of general government may fall short of providing for a full coverage of fiscal operations to the extent that it excludes the quasi-fiscal activities of state-owned financial institutions and nonfinancial enterprises. To account for direct or indirect govern-

---

[22]Relatively few IMF member countries can achieve this coverage on a timely basis; see International Monetary Fund (1995). Incomplete coverage is a major impediment for timely reporting under the IMF's SDDS. Of the 42 members that have so far subscribed to the SDDS, most have indicated that they will meet the request for up-to-date summary data on central government operations and debt, but about one-half may not be able to supply timely data on general government.

Box 2. Summary of Good Practices in Accounting Transparency

Coverage

General government, with sufficient detail on levels of government, and extrabudgetary funds (including social security institutions).

Quasi-fiscal activities of state-owned nonfinancial enterprises and financial institutions.

Recording basis

Accrual-based recording (including transactions in kind, cost of borrowing at a discount, and changes in arrears).

Supplementary cash-based recording.

Valuation and recognition

Measurement of government assets (including investment and depreciation).

Measurement of government liabilities outstanding.

Information on commitments and contingent (funded and unfunded) liabilities.

Estimates of net worth.

Classification

Breakdown of revenue categories.

Disaggregation of expenditure on an economic and functional basis.

Breakdown of debt and financing (by type, maturity, and creditor).

---

result in a misstatement of the magnitude and timing of fiscal operations. By comparison, the accrual-based approach is indispensable for gauging the macroeconomic resource repercussions of fiscal policy, especially over the medium to long term. Major distortions under cash-based recording stem from the exclusion of information on accumulation of arrears (especially expenditure arrears), transactions in kind (including issuance of government obligations to suppliers or tax refunds or in connection with bank restructuring), and the cost of borrowing at a discount. Although, increasingly, the accrual-based approach is seen as best practice, the presently more widespread cash-based government accounts should also be provided where both methods are possible.

The *valuation* and *recognition* of assets and liabilities can be critical for the transparency and consistency of government financial statements. In this regard, investment expenditure may be subject to varying treatment (full expensing or depreciation) depending on the analytical purpose at hand. Given the broader difficulties of valuing public assets, gross (rather than net) measurement of public debt is often preferable. Although attempts to estimate government net worth may ultimately prove successful, most countries are not yet in a position to prepare such estimates.

In addition, it is necessary to compile and disclose information on commitments and contingent liabilities. Examples of these liabilities are guarantees for credits extended by financial institutions and for deposits in those institutions, many of which are not quantifiable because they are contingent on the realization of the insured occurrence.[24] More important, they include obligations to future beneficiaries of social insurance for old-age, unemployment, and health care programs. Under accounting conventions followed in most countries, contingent liabilities for such benefit programs are not to be added to actual government debt. Thus, rather than being included in the government balance sheet, estimates of the net unfunded portion of these benefit-related contingent liabilities are generally published separately.[25]

Fiscal transparency requires *classifying* data on government operations, ownership, and liabilities into analytically useful categories of flows and stocks.

ment ownership of nonfinancial public enterprises, a number of countries report data for the nonfinancial public sector; others have expanded coverage to include official financial institutions, thereby encompassing the entire public sector. As a preferable alternative, the concept of *general government activity*[23] is intended to accurately capture the cost of all government functions, including quasi-fiscal activities conducted outside the general government. In the event that the cost of quasi-fiscal activities proves impossible to quantify, transparency would be served by at least listing such activities.

The recording basis of government transactions—namely, cash or accrual—has important implications for the transparency of fiscal performance. Reliance solely on the cash-based approach, although helpful for assessing the first-order impact of government borrowing on inflation and the external balance, can

---

[23]This definition has been proposed for the revised *Government Finance Statistics Manual*, in International Monetary Fund (1996a).

[24]Where these contingent liabilities can be reliably estimated, they may be included in published balance sheets. For example, in the balance sheets prepared for the United States, the authorities have sought to overcome these problems by developing techniques that permit estimates to be made of the accruing cost of government contingent liabilities arising from loan guarantees and insurance programs. See United States, Office of Management and Budget (1997).

[25]For example, in the United States, the budget documents include a separate actuarial calculation of the financial balance of the Social Security and the Medicare Trust Funds.

Revenue should be broken down into major tax and nontax categories and unrequited transfers, while financing, including privatization receipts, should be shown below the line.[26] Expenditure must be classified into major functional and economic categories, separating debt amortization from interest payments and placing the former as a below-the-line negative financing item. Finally, financing flows, as well as the corresponding debt stock, should be disaggregated by currency denomination, maturity, and source.

Indicators and Projections

The most commonly available *direct indicator* of the fiscal balance, namely, the overall balance of government operations, is transparent only to the extent that it is free of distortions in data coverage, recording, and classification. Although generally useful, the overall balance must be supplemented by alternative measures subject to the same transparency requirements (Box 3). Calculating the current balance, as an indicator of the government's contribution to national saving, requires a clear separation of current and capital transactions; this separation, in turn, depends on a satisfactory measurement of government investment expenditure. The primary balance, instrumental for determining the fiscal policy effort needed to stabilize or reduce public debt, requires exclusion of net interest payments from the overall balance. Measurement of the operational balance—in countries that have experienced high inflation and large levels of indebtedness—entails identifying interest payments and deducting the inflationary component of such interest outlays from the overall balance.

In addition to these flow indicators, most countries compile some direct indicator of the change in the stock of assets and liabilities. It is often argued that the net worth—calculated as the difference between the total stock of assets and liabilities—of the general government is a superior measure.[27] Given that most IMF members are unlikely to be able to compile such indicators in the short run, the next preferred alternative may be financial net worth, that is, the difference between the stock of financial assets and liabilities of the general government. However, in the absence of satisfactory data on financial assets, it is necessary to rely on gross debt mea-

---

[26]Under the proposed revision of the Government Finance Statistics (GFS) classification, privatization receipts are to be shown "below the line" as financing—thus removing the impact of such transactions from the measurement of the thrust of fiscal policy. This practice is in conformity with the System of National Accounts (SNA) definitions (Inter-Secretariat Working Group on National Accounts, 1993).

[27]For a summary of the arguments for and against the net worth concept, see Blejer and Cheasty (1993).

Box 3. Summary of Good Practices in Transparency of Indicators and Projections

Direct indicators

Overall balance, complemented by current, primary, and operational balances.

Gross and net government debt, accompanied by an estimate of net worth.

Analytical indicators

Structural or cyclically adjusted balance.

Sustainability calculations (showing primary balance required to stabilize debt, given realistic assumptions about future interest rates and GDP growth rates).

Present value of net unfunded liabilities (under contributory, defined-benefit social security programs); calculation of contribution gap.

Generational accounts.

Short- to medium-term forecasts

Separate baseline forecast and policy forecasts.

Clear and realistic underlying macroeconomic forecasts and parameters.

Long-term scenarios

Separate baseline scenario and adjustment scenarios (especially for old-age and health care programs).

Clear and realistic range of underlying macroeconomic parameters and demographic trends.

---

sures—usually the focus of financial markets (International Monetary Fund, 1996b).

To understand the direction of fiscal policy, the public and financial markets often find it useful to examine *analytical indicators* of the short-run fiscal stance. Perhaps the best known are indicators that remove the effect of cyclical fluctuations or exogenous shocks from direct measures of the budget balance. Given the underlying information required on macroeconomic developments and key fiscal parameters, indicators such as the structural balance are used predominantly in the advanced economies.

Another major question is whether persistent budget deficits result in a growth path for debt that is not sustainable. Long-run debt sustainability can be determined on the basis of an examination of current indebtedness levels, the interest rate, the GDP growth rate, and the ratio of the primary budget balance to GDP. In addition to explicit debt measures, it is useful to gauge the sustainability of the implicit government debt stemming from public pensions, health care benefits, and other defined-benefit programs. This assessment can be made by estimating the present value of net unfunded liabilities of these programs as a ratio of GDP. Another approach consists in calculating the contribution gap that would have to be met to make these programs sustainable.[28] Publication of such measures can help develop a widespread understanding of the need for structural reform to preserve or restore the sustainability of these schemes.

Increasing concern with the long-run distributional implications of the existing fiscal structure has also spawned the construction of generational accounts. One benefit of such accounts is that they often highlight the fact that policy changes can shift resources across generations without affecting the present fiscal deficit at all; however, largely because of their computational complexity, these accounts are available for only a few advanced economies with rapidly aging populations.[29]

---

[28]The contribution gap is the difference between a constant sustainable contribution that, over a long period of time, would not lead to a buildup of liabilities under public pension and other defined-benefit programs above an initial level and the expected average contribution rate likely to prevail under current law. See International Monetary Fund (1996b).

[29]In many cases, generational accounts are prepared by private sector analysts rather than governments, partly reflecting the judgmental assumptions often required to compile these estimates.

Formulation of fiscal policy, as well as the accompanying public debate on targets and strategy, is usually predicated on projections of future trends in government finances and in overall economic performance. Transparency in projections, whether model-based or judgmental, requires explicit, realistic, and timely assumptions, along with internal consistency. In the publication of short-run fiscal forecasts and the underlying macroeconomic forecasts, governments should provide baseline projections, which assume unchanged policies, and alternative projections, which incorporate the impact of major policy changes. Fiscal projections must be based on realistic and explicitly documented macroeconomic assumptions and parameters (e.g., effective tax rates, tax bases, compliance coefficients, or collection lags). Transparency is further assisted when the actual outcome is evaluated against projections.

Similarly, assessment of fiscal sustainability—in view of rapidly aging populations, the rising cost of health care, and the rigidity of most social entitlements—should be based on long-term scenarios, showing the evolution of the fiscal balance over several decades. Such scenarios can be particularly useful for ascertaining the sustainability of social security systems and illustrating, in a transparent manner, the effect of specific reform options.

III Role of the IMF in Promoting Fiscal Transparency

Major progress has been made throughout virtually the entire IMF membership toward fiscal transparency. The IMF has played a role in this endeavor through various channels: surveillance in the context of Article IV consultation discussions and World Economic Outlook (WEO) exercises; conditionality in IMF-supported programs; technical assistance, including training covering a wide range of public finance and statistical issues; development and publication of the Government Finance Statistics (GFS) Database; development of standards for data dissemination; publication of research on selected fiscal policy issues; and the recent initiative to promote good governance. For the most part, with the exception of technical assistance, IMF involvement has focused on fiscal transparency at the macroeconomic level, as well as on microeconomic issues (e.g., quasi-fiscal operations of public enterprises) that have direct macroeconomic repercussions.

Overall Trends and Priorities

In recent years, most IMF member countries have made important steps toward greater fiscal transparency.[30] To be sure, however, even the advanced economies exhibit some nontransparent arrangements and practices. The economies in transition—which until the beginning of the decade had conducted fiscal policy in virtual secrecy—have made the greatest leap toward transparency, although some of them still have among the least transparent fiscal systems. Considerable scope remains for eliminating nontransparent practices in many countries; nevertheless, it is important to keep in mind the distinction between unintended nontransparency attributable to slow technical and institutional development and deliberate misrepresentation or suppression of information. The latter, in principle, can be remedied over a shorter time horizon.

In the future, for the advanced economies, the main priority appears to lie in making public comprehensive information to facilitate the debate over fiscal discipline and debt sustainability issues. To this end, more precise specification of policy targets and subsequent monitoring of progress toward achieving them are required. These steps, in turn, presuppose increased attention to most measurement issues raised in the previous section, including those that bear on the intertemporal implications of fiscal policy—especially entitlement programs associated with aging. In particular, progress on these issues involves estimates of net unfunded liabilities and quasi-fiscal operations, costing of tax expenditures and regulation, and improved documentation of fiscal projections.

In the developing economies, attention should be focused on institutional reforms—enhancing transparency mainly in the budget process, taxation, and quasi-fiscal activities of public or private nonfinancial enterprises and financial institutions—and on the compilation and dissemination of essential fiscal data and projections. The economies in transition share many of the needs of developing countries, but their history of secrecy—including widespread quasi-fiscal activities and data systems oriented to planning rather than to market needs—may make it more difficult for them to move rapidly toward transparent fiscal practices. In many developing and transition economies, efforts in this area are particularly important for promoting good governance.

Role of the IMF

Article IV consultations provide the main vehicle for exercising surveillance over member country policies. In this context, the IMF must assess the intent and viability of fiscal adjustment programs largely on the basis of the underlying data and forecasts. The quality of the assessment therefore depends on the transparency of available information. Conversely, as part of this assessment, the IMF has often urged the authorities to increase transparency by, among other measures, eliminating or making explicit government expenditure and tax payment arrears, off-budget operations, and quasi-fiscal activities; removing nontransparent subsidies from commodity stabilization funds and public pension

---

[30]For a selection of country examples, see Appendix IV.

funds; and trimming or making apparent the cost of government regulation of labor, commodity, and financial markets. Fiscal policy advice at the individual country level has been supported by analysis in a multilateral context through the WEO exercises—drawing, in part, on internationally comparable measures of fiscal stance and sustainability for major advanced economies.

Conditionality in IMF-supported programs often requires implementation of fiscal policy advice in the form of prior actions, performance criteria, and structural benchmarks. Quantitative performance criteria for fiscal aggregates, including the budget balance, need to be transparent and based on the principles discussed above (Section II). In addition, the programs are normally to be cast in the framework of consistent medium-term fiscal adjustment scenarios.

At the request of member countries, the IMF's Fiscal Affairs Department has provided technical assistance over a wide range of public finance issues. Some of the recommendations offered through such assistance—with a view to promoting transparency—have included eliminating discretionary or negotiated tax preferences and hidden subsidy schemes, formulating budget framework laws, unifiying treasury accounts, establishing timely and comprehensive budget reporting systems[31] and public enterprise monitoring systems, improving fiscal forecasting, and developing long-term policy scenarios to simulate various pension and health care reform options. Often, these recommendations have been incorporated in IMF-supported programs or have served as inputs in Article IV consultation discussions. In addition, the IMF's Statistics Department has extended considerable assistance to improve government statistics on the basis of well-established accounting conventions.

A major effort in the promotion of fiscal transparency has been the development of the GFS methodology, its adoption by IMF member countries, and the construction and publication of the GFS Database. The current revision of the GFS guidelines, in line with the 1993 System of National Accounts (SNA) standards, represents a further step toward improving the transparency and consistency of fiscal statistics.[32] The recent creation of the IMF's Special Data Dissemination Standard (SDDS), aimed at countries accessing international capital markets, represents another important effort to promote transparency in the dissemination of macroeconomic data; fiscal databases are included, albeit on a highly aggregated basis.[33]

In recent years, transparency has been further served by the publication of research on selected fiscal policy issues, in the form of background papers for Article IV consultations and the semiannual *World Economic Outlook* reports. In addition, the recent publication of staff studies on the quasi-fiscal activities of public financial institutions, the fiscal implications of aging, and the fiscal costs of bank restructuring has contributed to the public's understanding of such issues. Most recently, the IMF has launched a major initiative to promote good governance in member countries, which involves, of course, increased fiscal transparency.

Overall, IMF advice and assistance in public finances, encompassing institutional arrangements, policy measures, administrative practices, statistical standards, and forecasting techniques, have made a major contribution to the current trend toward greater fiscal transparency.

Although considerable headway has been made toward transparency in government operations, there is ample scope for further progress in most member countries. Against this background, consideration is being given to extending IMF involvement—in cooperation with other multilateral institutions. In many countries, the IMF can build on the willingness of the authorities to move ahead rapidly with reforms. With some members providing examples of good practice, the IMF may play an increasing role as a catalyst, engendering interest in and information on good practice techniques to governments that show a desire for improvement.

---

[31]The World Bank (1994) has also provided assistance to increase transparency in the budget process in Africa, Asia, and Latin America.

[32]The revised GFS guidelines formally adopt an accrual-based recording method to supplement, rather than replace, the cash-based recording method currently used in many member countries (Appendix II). Operationally, accrual-based recording under the new guidelines can be achieved in these countries by compiling the additional information (on arrears and various noncash transactions) needed to complement existing cash data in instances where the differences between cash and accrual data are significant.

[33]The General Data Dissemination System, expected to be established soon, will promote transparency throughout the membership.

IV Summary and Conclusions

Fiscal transparency—defined as public openness in government institutions, fiscal policy intentions, public sector accounts, indicators, and forecasts—is fundamental to sound economic policy. Transparency allows the market to evaluate, and impose discipline on, government policy and increases the political risk of unsustainable policies. The potential role of transparency in promoting good governance has been widely recognized.

Despite the inherent difficulty of fully corroborating the link between transparency, on the one hand, and fiscal discipline and economic performance, on the other, it can be shown that the better-performing countries in the various major regions of IMF membership generally follow more transparent fiscal practices. There are good reasons to believe that fiscal transparency contributes to macroeconomic stability, allocative efficiency, and fairness. Furthermore, fiscal transparency leads to increased credibility, which, in turn, helps reduce risk premiums in financial markets and strengthens support by the electorate. Notwithstanding this general presumption, a temporary departure from transparency may sometimes be justified—notably, when the premature announcement of sensitive statistical data or policy measures would weaken their effectiveness and confer unintended windfall gains on some groups.

A review of issues in fiscal transparency points to the importance of adopting practices and providing information that ensure a clear demarcation between the public and private sectors. This includes documentation and quantification of the extent of government intervention in such areas as bank rescue and enterprise restructuring operations and privatization. Also, information should be made available on the cost of any quasi-fiscal activities of state-owned or private nonfinancial enterprises and financial institutions. Unless there is a clear economic rationale for placing certain activities off-budget, governments should refrain from doing so. In any event, sufficient information on such activities should be provided to ensure that they are subject to the same public and legislative scrutiny as on-budget operations. The budget process should involve, above all, public disclosure of budget documents—including clear enunciation of fiscal targets and strategies—and open legislative debate. Transparency in budget execution and control includes open procurement, contracting, and hiring practices. Financial and performance audits of budget operations should be subject to public scrutiny. In the tax area, transparency entails clearly defined statutes, with no recourse to discretionary tax concessions or negotiated tax liabilities. Published tax expenditure estimates should underpin debates on the draft budget or on tax reform. Information should be made available on the terms and sources of government deficit financing. Similarly, the criteria and terms of government lending should be clearly disclosed. Recent gains from deregulation should be consolidated with the implementation of a simple regulatory framework that can be costed transparently.

Sound fiscal policymaking requires clarity in the measurement of government transactions, ownership, and obligations. To this end, coverage of fiscal accounts should extend to the entire general government, supplemented with information on quasi-fiscal activities, preferably applying accrual-based recording. In practice, cash-based recording—useful for short-run fiscal analysis—can be enhanced with data on payment arrears, transactions in kind, and discount securities to approximate an accrual-based presentation, which is necessary to determine the medium-term implications of budget policy. Other issues that have a bearing on the transparency of government accounts are the appropriate valuation of assets and liabilities—including recognition of commitments and contingent liabilities—and a meaningful classification of revenue, expenditure, and debt.

Transparency is also necessary for indicators of fiscal stance and sustainability. Various measures of government balance and public indebtedness must be disclosed. Also, calculation of the actuarial value of net unfunded entitlement liabilities and estimates of generational accounts are useful. Publication of fiscal projections should be documented with sufficient information on the underlying methodology and key macroeconomic assumptions. Explicit medium-term fiscal projections need to be incorporated in annual budget documents. In countries with rapidly aging populations, long-term scenarios for public pension and health care programs should be published regularly. Moreover, the government should make public a retrospective evaluation of the actual outcome against projections.

Although, in recent years, many IMF member countries have made substantial progress toward transparency in virtually all these areas, there is considerable scope for improvement. Advanced economies should concentrate on developing more transparent measures of fiscal sustainability, along with an open debate of reform options in the face of aging populations. In developing economies, emphasis should be on promoting transparency in government institutions and on disseminating essential fiscal data and projections. In the economies in transition, adoption of new attitudes is essential to support the institution-building process.

The case for eliminating the remaining nontransparent practices is underscored by the vulnerability of the world economy to the increasing integration of financial markets across country boundaries. Transparency in public finances can contribute to policy credibility and thus help prevent a potential crisis from materializing and spreading across countries. At the same time, it is important to recognize that greater transparency may involve costs, particularly where information systems and reporting practices have to be developed or improved; and that efforts to promote fiscal openness must enjoy strong support in member countries if they are to succeed.

The IMF has contributed to the improvement in fiscal transparency in most areas through surveillance, program design and implementation, technical assistance, development and application of statistical standards, and publication of research activities. However, at least until recently, these efforts did not always translate into enhanced fiscal transparency by member governments toward their own electorate and financial markets. The recent establishment of the Special Data Dissemination Standard—to promote transparency mainly in macroeconomic databases—is a potentially important initiative in this regard. In addition, further steps are being considered to strengthen the role of the IMF in promoting fiscal transparency.

Appendix I   Transparency in Institutions and Behavior

Transparency in government behavior is reflected mainly in the structure and functions of the public sector, and particularly in the budget process, tax treatment, financing operations, and regulatory mechanism. This appendix focuses on the broad range of fiscal arrangements that determine the frontier between the public and private sectors in these areas. In addition, it examines the functions of, and interactions among, various components of the government as well as their relationship with the rest of the public sector.

Overall Structure and Functions

Transparency in the boundary between the public sector and private economic agents entails development of a well-defined and publicly available policy statement that sets the relative areas of competence and provides limited, if any, scope for private rent seeking in the public domain. Apart from some areas (e.g., education, health care, and public utilities) where public and private providers may operate concurrently, in most industrial countries and some developing countries, the separation between public and private activity has been clarified over the past two decades. While the government has retained responsibility for public administration, internal safety, defense, foreign relations, and macroeconomic policy, the private sector has become the principal actor in commercial and profit-making activities and, in some cases, infrastructure.

Recently, certain industrial countries have taken steps to conduct the remaining government operations by applying more explicit cost and performance indicators and management techniques used by private enterprises.[34] But the marked increase in the outsourcing of government operations to large-scale private suppliers or contractors (in areas such as defense, health care, and certain administrative services), whose principal or sole client is the government, may offer scope for nontransparent behavior, even if the transactions are formally subject to open

tender.[35] Whereas the boundaries between public and private spheres are generally weaker in developing than in industrial countries,[36] the demarcation is perhaps least transparent in the economies in transition. In these economies, for the most part, the boundaries have not yet been defined—lacking even conflict-of-interest legislation—to the point where, in some countries, public officials are allowed to engage in transactions for personal profit using public resources, including internal government information.

Freedom-of-information legislation is another fundamental instrument of government transparency and accountability.[37] It gives citizens access to government documents without their first having to prove a special interest, and the burden of justifying nondisclosure falls on the government. Although such legislation imposes administrative costs, and exempting highly sensitive issues in certain areas (e.g., defense and foreign affairs) can be justified, experience suggests that it can change the attitude of elected officials and civil servants toward fiscal transparency.

Within the public sector, publicly released information on the assignment of functions among various components of the sector is not always available and, when available, is not always clear, even in some advanced economies. The nexus between the government and public financial institutions or nonfinancial public enterprises is rather opaque in many cases.[38] The paucity of publicly available informa-

---

[34]See the examples cited in Gore (1993, p. 76).

[35]See, for example, Gansler (1995) on U.S. defense expenditures.

[36]Sometimes, the boundaries between the activities of the state and those of its political leaders are by no means transparent. For example, in some countries, the differences between public resources and the personal finances of the ruling family are often not explicitly articulated.

[37]The earliest legislation governing the opening of government records to the public dates back to 1776 in Sweden. The present law is unique in that it is one of the four laws that together make up Sweden's Constitution. Similar, but less rigorous, systems were introduced in the 1970s in Denmark, Finland, Norway, and the United States. Since then, legislation on open records has spread to most industrial countries; see Pope (1996).

[38]In France, for example, Morin and Dupuy (1993) have argued that both the extent of subsidization and the degree of state involvement in public enterprises lack transparency.

tion on the fiscal costs and the terms of bank rescue operations (Alexander and others, 1997) and of enterprise restructuring has been notable, not only in virtually all economies in transition but also in some industrial and developing countries. In some cases, financial injections were provided in an ad hoc manner, often from off-budget sources.[39] The privatization of state-owned enterprises has been conducted with varying degrees of openness across countries. In some countries (e.g., Australia, most EU countries, New Zealand, and United States), there has been nearly full public disclosure on all aspects of enterprise sale.[40]

Notwithstanding the general trend toward managing and operating state-owned enterprises in an increasingly open way along commercial lines (e.g., Australia and New Zealand)—in some cases, in preparation for eventual privatization—state-owned enterprises in a number of countries are still engaged in sizable quasi-fiscal activities, mainly in the form of social benefits, overemployment, and price subsidies without compensation from the budget.[41] Such quasi-fiscal activities are remnants of the widespread provision of implicit subsidies for consumption of loosely defined "merit" goods and services and for employment, not only in the former centrally planned economies but also in many developing countries.[42] Although the ideal solution would be to phase out such activities over time, transparency requires that estimates of their costs be published in budget documents.

Perhaps less transparent are the quasi-fiscal activities conducted by public financial institutions. These activities take many different forms: multiple exchange rates, exchange rate guarantees, import deposits, preferential credits and loan guarantees (directed, e.g., to exports, and investment in specific activities), deposit guarantees, and selective reserve requirements (Mackenzie and Stella, 1996). Such implicit subsidies and taxes, not explicitly remunerated by the government, can be found especially in developing and transition economies. Again, as a first step, it is necessary to improve the transparency of these operations through the publication of estimates of the costs involved.

A lack of clarity in the division of responsibilities between national and subnational levels of government is a major problem in many developing and transition economies and, to a lesser degree, in some industrial countries. Although revenue sharing has been clarified in some countries, including those with clear formula-based arrangements (e.g., Canada and Denmark), in others, bargaining and ad hoc negotiations persist for intergovernmental transfers. The least transparent distribution of functions and resources can be found, of course, in some economies in transition that have recently evolved from a highly centralized system of government to a federation or confederation.

In principle, extrabudgetary operations can be useful for pursuing certain tasks more efficiently (or for ensuring greater support from users) on a fiduciary basis, in the form of separate funds—though often administered in a manner similar to budget entities—particularly if their spending obligation transcends the annual budget appropriation process. Such is the case for highway funds (established for road construction and maintenance and financed from earmarked user fees and capital transfers), commodity stabilization funds (set up to mitigate the effect of export price fluctuations), or social insurance funds (to protect against unemployment, old age, or disability).[43] In a number of countries, however, extrabudgetary funds—for example, to finance export promotion, tourism, housing, and, in particular, military expenditures—have apparently been created, at least in part, to avoid legislative scrutiny. Often, extrabudgetary funds that were originally created for valid reasons have become highly dysfunctional. In some African countries, reserves accumulated in commodity stabilization funds have been diverted to finance consumer subsidies or prestige projects. Instead of relying on active labor-market programs or deregulation, a number of European and Latin American countries (except under defined-contribution schemes) use social security funds as a nontransparent means for alleviating structural unemployment, through easy eligibility for old-age and disability pensions. In some countries, reform efforts are under way to limit early retirement and excessive use of disability benefits and sick pay. Although efforts to do away with such dysfunctional practices should be stepped up, the immediate task is to make the activities of these funds transparent through publication of their operations on a timely basis and in a manner that permits consolidation with budget operations.

---

[39]For example, in the United States, until 1992, the rescue of failed savings and loan institutions was treated off-budget.

[40]Other examples where transparency prevailed in certain aspects of privatization include mass distribution of state-owned enterprises (Czech Republic); earmarking of the bulk of proceeds for debt reduction (Hungary); and rapid and open marketing of assets held (former German Democratic Republic).

[41]In practice, such uncompensated quasi-fiscal operations tend to go hand in hand with tax exemptions, deferments of tax payments, and other tax concessions.

[42]See the discussion of such practices in former centrally planned economies in Kopits (1991) and Tanzi (1993).

---

[43]Examples of well-functioning funds are the U.S. Highway Trust Fund; Chile's Copper Compensatory Fund; and the U.S. Old-Age, Survivors', and Disability Insurance trust funds. See also Potter (1997).

One potentially important instrument for ensuring transparency in government operations is a permanent independent review agency that is responsible for conducting studies on selected fiscal issues, performance audits—focusing on the efficiency and effectiveness of government programs—and appraisals of the activities of specific public sector institutions, including state-owned enterprises. Such an agency, accountable to the legislature and the public at large, can be found in most industrial countries, some developing countries, and a few economies in transition.[44] Occasionally, some governments commission outside experts to prepare special studies—such as white papers on selected policy issues in Commonwealth countries that contain detailed factual assessments and nonbinding recommendations for reform.

Budgetary Practices

The budget process, undertaken under varying degrees of transparency, normally comprises four main stages: formulation and preparation of the draft budget, legislation and approval, budget execution, and audit and review. In some countries (e.g., Germany and Switzerland), including an increasing number of economies in transition, the tasks involved at each stage are detailed in the budget framework law. In others (e.g., United Kingdom), the process has been set by past conventions and rulings. In either case, the process can be said to be transparent if it follows clearly established guidelines rather than an improvised approach, is fully explained, openly debated and enacted, and applied preferably to the entire general government, including extrabudgetary operations and local governments.

The first stage—preparation of the draft budget—involves internal debate and resolution of priorities within the government. Although the actual formulation of budget proposals is an internal matter, the timetable and decision-making process used by the government should be publicly known. Of course, once completed, the budget and the supporting documents (such as the budget speech and various specialized analyses) need to be published and made widely available in an understandable and meaningful format. Clear announcement of the fiscal target embodied in the budget documents is seen as one of the most important aspects of transparency because,

by analogy with the inflation targets used in monetary policy, it conditions the expectations of private and public sector participants.[45]

Following formal presentation of the budget, government representatives are responsible for explaining—as openly and in as much detail as necessary—its contents and the underlying rationale and policies, often at legislative hearings. By their nature, the actual legislative debate and authorization are normally open to the public, and the outcome is recorded in public documents that become the foundation for the next stage. The execution stage requires both internal transparency (timely monitoring of information on actual spending and cash movements through the treasury) and external transparency (prompt reporting to the public). Finally, adequate information is to be made available for conducting both financial and performance audits, and the results, including any actions recommended and implemented, are to be disclosed to the public.[46]

Whereas the foregoing transparency criteria are formally met in most countries that have separate executive and legislative branches, the quality of information is often inadequate. Moreover, the specification of fiscal targets, particularly medium-term targets,[47] incorporated in the annual budget document is in many cases vague. The linkage between these targets and actual policy measures, on the one hand, and ultimate economic goals, on the other, is often unclear. A major problem stems from the reporting on the realization (or nonrealization) of fiscal targets. Many governments, especially in nonindustrial countries, fail to explain fiscal developments in the course of the year; thus, public knowledge of slippages is delayed. Added weaknesses in budget execution transparency stem from information lags and incomplete

---

[44]Examples are Australia's Auditor General, the United Kingdom's National Audit Office, the United States General Accounting Office, and Hungary's Office of State Audit. In France, reviewing and monitoring are carried out under the authority of the Interministerial Evaluation Committee. However, in a number of Latin American countries, the comptroller general is responsible only for legal and financial audits.

[45]The innovations introduced in New Zealand (Appendix IV) instructing the government to declare fiscal targets consistent with a set of prudent principles, enshrined in the Fiscal Responsibility Act, is an example of a high level of transparency. Recently, Australia adopted the Charter of Budget Honesty, requiring, among other things, clear announcement of fiscal targets and intergenerational analysis of fiscal policies. Although all member countries of the Organization for Economic Cooperation and Development (OECD) and a number of other countries have adopted fiscal targets in one form or another, many are poorly specified and lack policy relevance in that they cannot be easily related to general economic goals (such as debt stabilization and desired national savings levels). See Organization for Economic Cooperation and Development (1995a) for a critique.

[46]Although performance reviews (including quantitative performance indicators) of specific agency programs may also be published, for many governments this is largely an internal matter that feeds into the preparation of the subsequent budget. Thus, the review reports may be attached to the budget documents and can justify the proposed expansion or reduction in specific allocations.

[47]For an overview of multiyear budgets and targets in OECD countries, see Organization for Economic Cooperation and Development (1995a) and Appendix III.

coverage, mostly in developing countries and economies in transition. It is perhaps most difficult to achieve transparency in budget audit and review. Although a number of Asian countries (e.g., India and Korea) have made considerable strides toward openness, some other countries in the region and in Africa still exhibit nontransparency at various stages of the budget process.[48] Despite taking some important steps to shed a tradition of secrecy, most economies in transition (with the exception of a few Central European countries) need to make further progress toward transparency in the budget process as a whole.

In response to unanticipated exogenous developments, most industrial countries follow clear guidelines for using contingency reserves (e.g., Australia and United Kingdom), resorting to cash limits (e.g., formerly in the United Kingdom), or preparing a supplementary budget. By contrast, many economies in transition rely widely on discretionary steps, including sequestration of entitlements, often to contain an unbudgeted widening of the deficit in the course of the fiscal year.

A further test of transparency in budget execution and control involves public procurement, contracting, and employment practices. In the majority of OECD member countries—at the national rather than at subnational government levels—public tenders are issued for major government contracts, procurement of supplies above a certain threshold are subject to open bidding, and awards are publicly announced.[49] Overall, there is increasing reliance in these countries on the contracting out of basic government services. Similarly, a number of countries that previously operated closed career systems have introduced open recruitment. Although some progress has also been made in Latin America (e.g., Chile and Venezuela) toward increased transparency in this area, in many developing countries, there is considerable room for discretionary purchasing practices and patronage in the civil service.[50] The lack of transparency in the

economies in transition[51] is not surprising, given a background of completely internal procurement practices—especially during the shortages that prevailed under central planning—and of hiring under the *nomenklatura* system.

Tax Treatment

In general, a transparent tax system is characterized by relatively small differences between statutory and effective tax rates on transactions, income, and property. The extent of such differences is determined by tax evasion, administrative shortcomings, or tax concessions. Hence, to reduce the differences, the tax base should be well defined, and modifications through preferential treatment should be based on clear statutory criteria of eligibility. Also, tax administration should be conducted in a clear and simple manner, assisted by dissemination of all the necessary information, including instructions for completing tax returns. Discretionary tax relief provided to particular individuals or enterprises (including state-owned enterprises), as practiced in some developing countries and virtually all economies in transition, constitutes a departure from transparency. In these countries as well as in a few industrial countries, taxpayers are able to accumulate substantial tax or social security contribution arrears, or overdue obligations, subject to almost endless litigation—in some cases, even with tacit government approval. Least transparent, however, is the case-by-case negotiation of tax liabilities between tax officials and corporate taxpayers, which has been made available mainly to foreign investors in many developing countries. In some of these countries, however, as well as in economies in transition, this approach has proliferated.

As a step toward transparent tax administration, most of the advanced economies have promulgated laws or statutes specifying taxpayers' rights and obligations (Organization for Economic Cooperation and Development, 1990). Obligations include filing tax returns and making tax payments by the due date; and filing information returns on wages, interest income, or payments for merchandise made by third parties. Likewise, the authority to impose penalties, including the search and seizure of assets, is legally defined. In many countries, tax officials are obliged to adhere to strictly enforced rules of conduct; taxpayers who have the right to privacy may turn to the administration or to the courts for protection from arbitrary treatment. In some countries, taxpayers may appeal to a tax referee; the legal costs are covered if the taxpayer's appeal is success-

---

[48]Although progress is being achieved in a number of African countries, where budgets are required to be openly debated in national assemblies.

[49]In countries such as Australia, Canada, New Zealand, the United Kingdom, and the United States, these practices are highly visible. Recently, EU members have been required to adopt uniform procurement standards. The development of open-tender practices across country borders has been stimulated by standards set by the World Trade Organization. The OECD has also played an important role in propagating such practices.

[50]The World Bank and other multilateral agencies have actively promoted improvements in these areas. One potentially promising initiative in the procurement area is the "Islands of Integrity" approach pursued by Transparency International, a nonprofit organization. Under this scheme, endorsed by the World Bank, Transparency International monitors the bidding for public contracts; if either party—the national authorities or a bidder—is found to engage in corrupt practices, that party is excluded from any subsequent bidding.

[51]As an exception, effective in 1996, Hungary began applying procurement standards compatible with those adopted by the EU.

ful. Such a clear definition and enforcement of rules and regulations are absent in many developing countries and most economies in transition.

Tax preferences can be viewed as tantamount to budgetary outlays benefiting households or specific economic sectors or activities. For this reason, estimates of tax expenditures—that is, loss of revenue compared with the level that would obtain in the absence of tax allowances—can provide valuable information to the legislature and the public, particularly at the time of the annual budget debate or during tax reform, despite the difficulty of defining the reference value for each tax expenditure category. At present, one dozen OECD member countries regularly publish expenditure accounts that show the estimated budgetary cost of tax exemptions, deductions, credits, deferrals, and reduced rates.[52]

Similarly, useful information about the distributional implications of a country's tax subsidy system can be gleaned from incidence studies, albeit with some methodological and measurement limitations, including those associated with the underlying household budget surveys. In some industrial countries (e.g., Australia), the government periodically publishes tax subsidy incidence calculations, often prepared under contract by nongovernmental organizations. In addition, of course, it would be informative to occasionally estimate differences among statutory, effective, and realized tax rates—especially for taxes on company income and foreign trade.[53]

Financing Operations

Besides its adverse monetary and macroeconomic consequences, nonmarket bank financing of government deficits also conceals the true cost of debt servicing. For this reason, in the past two decades, an increasing number of countries have resorted to market-based, nonbank financing of deficits, accompanied by a parallel effort to create an arm's-length relationship between governments on the one hand and central banks and other financial institutions on the other. Thus, apart from a few economies in transition and some developing countries, public financial institutions are no longer a captive source of

deficit financing at below-market interest rates. However, such practices still account at least partially for the domestic borrowing requirement of the public sector in certain large countries.

The trend toward market-based financing operations has enhanced transparency and received the support of financial markets. In fact, governments wishing to access international markets must furnish rating agencies, underwriters, and security market supervisory agencies with considerable data on their debt stock, including guarantees, debt-service capacity, and overall debt-management strategy—as well as information on macroeconomic developments and outlook. For successful domestic financing, governments need to provide information on marketing techniques, the mix of domestic and external maturity structure and other characteristics of securities to be issued, and rules governing public tenders and open market operations.

Nonetheless, certain subtle nontransparent debt-management practices can be found in some industrial and developing countries. For instance, strong moral suasion by the authorities on institutional investors and discretionary selection of underwriters, financing consortiums, and primary dealers are examples of less visible practices. In addition, insufficient or excessively complex public information on the terms of acquisition or sale of various types of government securities, coupled with a lack of adequate retail outlets or secondary markets, may constrain proper risk evaluation and, hence, the development of markets for such instruments. In countries with regulated markets, transparency would be served by providing estimates of the cost of such restraints in budget documents to show the degree of subsidization and consequent resource misallocation introduced by such practices.

In government lending, the least transparent practices prevail in some economies in transition and parts of Asia and the Middle East, where the authorities allocate credit directly.[54] On-lending by governments or by public (or, in some cases, private) financial institutions, often through government guarantee, can be equally nontransparent.

Regulation

Government regulation is often justified for a variety of objectives: public health, consumer protection, environmental protection, labor protection, and moral hazard prevention. In many countries, however, the complexity, overlapping jurisdictions (between na-

---

[52]In Austria, Belgium, France, Portugal, Spain, and the United States, the government is legally obliged to prepare an annual tax expenditure report, whereas in Australia and Germany, reports are prepared twice a year; see Organization for Economic Cooperation and Development (1996c).

[53]See, for example, Kyrouz (1975) and King and Fullerton (1984) on company income taxation. Whereas realized (average) rates are calculated from actual tax revenue as a proportion of actual income or transaction flows, effective (marginal) tax rates are estimated on an economically meaningful base (e.g., user cost of capital or required rate of return).

[54]In China, for example, the consolidated budget deficit for 1995 is to be adjusted upward by about 5 percent of GDP when policy lending by public financial institutions is included.

tional and subnational levels), frequent changes, and sheer volume of regulations all contribute to a lack of clarity in the regulatory framework. Moreover, regulations are sometimes used as a nontransparent substitute for budget transfers or taxes. For example, rent controls can be viewed as a substitute for transfers to low-income households; zoning regulations, obligatory military service, and training requirements for employers are substitutes for various forms of taxation (Tanzi, 1995). Similar substitution can also arise when a government department or agency (e.g., department of forestry) is responsible for both regulation and budget spending, given that managers may face conflicting pressures to achieve fiscal savings through the use of (less transparent) regulation.

Unlike public services financed from the budget, the costs of complying with regulations, some borne directly by the regulated households and enterprises and some borne indirectly by the rest of the economy, are not transparent. An attempt to assess these costs suggests that the extent of nontransparency in regulation can be considerable, especially in industrial countries.[55] In developing and transition economies, with greater latitude for evading regulations through the informal sector, these direct costs tend to be offset, at least in part, by costs associated with payoffs to the regulators themselves and to intermediaries who assist in evasion.

In general, the recent—practically worldwide—trend toward deregulation in commodity, labor, and financial markets has contributed to greater transparency in government operations in these areas. Although difficult to quantify, considerable progress toward deregulation has been attained by a number of advanced economies (e.g., Denmark, New Zealand, United Kingdom, and United States).[56] In some of these countries, however, there is a risk that these gains may be undone by renewed substitution of regulation for fiscal measures. While some developing countries in East Asia and Latin America (e.g., Chile) have embarked on major deregulation efforts, most economies in transition have made an impressive evolution from central planning—arguably the most overregulated system.

---

[55]According to Hopkins (1996), in the United States, the direct costs of federal regulation since 1992 have been estimated at about 9 percent of GDP, equivalent to nearly one-half of federal budget outlays.

[56]See Organization for Economic Cooperation and Development (1992) and Koedjik and Kremers (1996). Within the EU there has been considerable progress toward harmonizing regulations, but not always toward achieving greater transparency.

Appendix II   Transparency in Public Accounts

Transparency in the measurement of government transactions, ownership, and obligations rests on a set of basic attributes: institutional coverage, recording basis, valuation, and classification of flows and stocks. This appendix highlights those country practices that are consistent with, or deviate from, acceptable standards. Although in many respects they are indistinguishable from those applied in the private sector, these standards must conform primarily to the requirements of fiscal policy analysis. In assessing transparency in measurement, one must keep in mind the limitations of human capital in agencies charged with compiling government finance statistics, especially in some developing economies and economies in transition.

Coverage

In principle, the general government is universally regarded as the most comprehensive definition of the sector that "performs primarily the functions of supplying certain public goods and services and fulfilling certain public purposes not for commercial or financial reasons, or, if of a commercial or financial nature, not on a major basis or not primarily for a profit" (International Monetary Fund, 1986, p. 7). Its coverage encompasses the national (central) government consolidated with all subnational (provincial, municipal, or local) governments, consisting of the budget, as well as social security and other extrabudgetary accounts, at each level of government. Although nearly all countries can supply up-to-date information on the central budget—which for many is the main focus of policy—only in about two-thirds of the member countries of the Organization for Economic Cooperation and Development (OECD) are timely data for the consolidated general government available on a yearly basis.[57]

Many countries, including some major ones, do not provide comprehensive and timely information on ex-trabudgetary activities. Particular shortcomings include the inconsistency and lags in social security data in countries where such institutions enjoy a high degree of autonomy. Moreover, because the data on the operations of subnational governments have not been compiled and consolidated with those of the central government in a timely fashion, full coverage of the general government has not been possible. For some countries, large and small, the sheer number of subnational governments poses a major problem. For others, consolidation is made difficult by the need to attribute a large number of hard-to-identify intergovernmental fiscal transfers to grantor or recipient levels of governments. Also, data collection may be inhibited by legal restraints or by the complexities associated with the interposition of an additional regional or provincial tier of government in the subnational structure. However, in some developing countries and economies in transition, the main difficulty stems from the lack of consistent recording and from delays in information, which, in turn, can be traced largely to the shortage of well-developed financial management systems at the subnational level.

Further evidence of the difficulty of providing full and timely coverage is that in 1995 only 40 IMF member countries supplied internationally comparable information on consolidated central government accounts for the most recent year; an additional 30 members provided data with a one-year lag; another 32, with a lag of two or more years; and 13 provided recent data covering only the central budget. Of these 115 countries, 45 report timely data on social security institutions, and fewer than 20 provide up-to-date information on subnational government operations.[58]

In practice, even the general government falls short of full coverage of fiscal operations because it

---

[57]Such data are published in Organization for Economic Cooperation and Development (1996b) for 14 countries for the most recent year, for 3 countries with a one-year lag, and for 4 countries with a lag of two or more years.

[58]See International Monetary Fund (1995). Incomplete coverage of general government is a major impediment to timely reporting under the IMF's Special Data Dissemination Standard. Of the 42 members that intend to participate in the Special Data Dissemination Standard, most have indicated that they will meet the request for up-to-date summary data on central government operations and debt, but about one-half may not be able to supply timely data on general government.

excludes quasi-fiscal activities (including the cost of regulations) of public financial institutions and nonfinancial enterprises. To account fully for direct or indirect government ownership of nonfinancial public enterprises, some countries, particularly in South America (e.g., Brazil, Peru, and Venezuela), publicly report data for the nonfinancial public sector; others (e.g., Costa Rica, New Zealand, Portugal, and United Kingdom) have expanded coverage to official financial institutions as well, that is, encompassing the entire public sector.[59] Albeit a step in the right direction, this broad coverage may be viewed as a rough approximation of the true magnitude of government functions, whether undertaken inside or outside the general government sector. In fact, such coverage cannot be used to identify the source of losses incurred by public enterprises or financial institutions, which may reflect a cyclical downturn or poor business decisions, or, alternatively, the cost of quasi-fiscal activities. However, in a significant number of developing countries and economies in transition, there is little, if any, public reporting of quasi-fiscal activities by the state-owned enterprise sector or financial sector.

The concept of general government activity, proposed in the revised *Government Finance Statistics Manual*, is intended to accurately capture the cost of all government functions, including quasi-fiscal activities conducted outside the general government.[60] Although still at a conceptual stage, this coverage would provide a useful complement to institutionally based measures of general government and deserves widespread application in the future. However, the measure does not remove the need to separately cost quasi-fiscal activities whenever possible. If these activities prove impossible to quantify,[61] listing them would aid transparency.

Recording Basis

How government transactions are recorded, namely, on a cash or an accrual basis, is critical for the transparency of fiscal performance. On a cash basis, transactions are recorded when financial receipts or payments actually take place, even if there is no associated real economic flow.[62] This approach can be useful for two reasons. First, it is preferred for short-run budgetary control and analysis. Whereas it may be difficult to alter budget commitments or payment obligations in the short run, it may be relatively easy to record and monitor cash payments through treasury operations or, for example, to enhance revenue through an accelerated sale of assets. Second, cash-based accounts have been used traditionally to assess the first-order financial impact of the government borrowing requirement, if monetized, on inflation and on the external balance. By contrast, on an accrual basis, all economic transactions are recorded as they occur, regardless of whether the transaction is an in-kind or a for-cash payment.[63] Because transactions are recorded when they reflect changes in government assets and/or liabilities, including depreciation of plant and equipment, this approach permits full consistency between the government's income statement and balance sheet.[64] Accordingly, accrual-based accounts are indispensable for gauging the macroeconomic repercussions of fiscal policy—as well as the resource implications for the management of specific government programs—especially over the medium to long term.

In practice, neither the cash nor the accrual method needs to be adopted in a pure form; indeed, some countries find it attractive to pursue a modified cash or a modified accrual approach.[65] In countries that rely on the cash approach alone, the recording of certain important government transactions can be either distorted or nonexistent. Major areas where nontransparency may arise would be the exclusion of information on the accumulation of arrears, transactions in kind, and the cost of borrowing at a discount.

Measurement of revenue and expenditure arrears has become a problem, especially in countries where the tax or social security administration may face legal or political impediments in collecting taxes or payroll contributions, or where cash limits or se-

---

[59]Among these countries, only New Zealand has applied the formal consolidation rules required for "whole of government" reporting.

[60]According to International Monetary Fund (1996a, p. 12), the concept "includes all government functions carried out by general government units and units outside the general government sector and excludes nongovernment functions carried out by general government units."

[61]For example, the cost of sectoral credit ceilings used for directing credit to specific activities would require calculating implicit taxes and subsidies relative to an unconstrained outcome. According to estimates in Tanzi (1995), the cost of financial suppression through regulation in past years amounted to as much as 40 percent of total revenue in Mexico and 20 percent in India and Pakistan.

[62]A variant of the accrual basis is the due-for-payment basis, whereby the transaction is recorded when receipt or payment falls due.

[63]Specifically, recording takes place at the time economic value is created, transformed, exchanged, transferred, or extinguished.

[64]For a discussion of the usefulness of accrual-based government accounting, see Efford (1996) and International Federation of Accountants (1997).

[65]For instance, under a modified cash approach, changes in floating debt can be shown as a memorandum item. In another example, under a modified accrual approach, only payment or tax arrears within a certain time limit are recorded in the financial statement. See the general treatment in International Federation of Accountants (1995, 1997).

questration of funds is used to contain expenditures.[66] Exclusion of expenditure (tax) arrears leads to an understatement (overstatement) of government deficits.[67] Cash-based recording can, of course, be supplemented with memorandum items showing changes in floating debt that account for the difference between payment orders (tax liabilities incurred) and cash or checks issued (collected). However, payment orders issued often do not cover the full range of commitments made, and it may not be feasible to eliminate normal lags in processing checks; hence, floating debt cannot be regarded as a measure of genuine arrears.

Transactions in kind include certain grants and loans extended by one country to another and, sometimes, by one level of government to another; grants are more important in developing countries, and loans are more important in transition economies. Through such operations, a donor country may purchase goods and services and then pass them directly to the recipient or pay an outside commercial supplier to provide goods and services on its behalf.[68] In addition, barter transactions, which were frequent among former centrally planned economies (and vis-à-vis their free market trading partners), still occur occasionally in some economies in transition. Other noncash transactions include the issuance of government obligations—often in the form of securities—as payment for services received from suppliers, which, in turn, can be used to offset tax arrears or for tax refunds due to taxpayers; in a different context, tax arrears were written off with the transfer of equity to the government. In each case, the immediate effect of the transaction is an understatement of the true deficit.

A nontransparent accounting practice may arise in connection with noncash issuance of government debt, particularly in bank restructuring. Regardless of the recording basis, all interest payments involved in the bank recapitalization are to be shown as government expenditures. But under the accrual approach, the principal component of transferred government paper (less the market value of any nonperforming loans assumed by the government), if it is not accompanied by an increase in government equity, should also be recorded as expenditure. In either case, the net value of the transfer would contribute to an increase in government net debt. While always recording interest payments as expenditure, a number of countries have failed to show the principal component of the net value of bond transfers as expenditure. (For a review of country experiences, see Alexander and others, 1997.) Under this principle, any government debt issued in exchange for previous outstanding doubtful liabilities, including arrears, should be recorded as an expenditure in the amount of the difference in value between the new debt and the old debt.[69]

Several governments issue discount securities, with a zero or a low coupon rate of interest. The transparency implications of these securities under cash recording depend on the exact formulation of interest and repayment terms. In most cases, governments can permanently reduce the cash measure of interest payments. The cost of the borrowing is instead placed "below the line" as amortization payments. In some formulations, amortization can also be delayed by requiring a "bullet" repayment at maturity. A similar understatement of interest cost may take place with bonds that carry a fixed interest rate, although the principal is indexed to inflation with the effect of understating cash expenditures.[70] In all these situations, under accrual-based recording, all interest charges, including the indexation component, whether paid at maturity or not, would be shown continuously during the life of the instrument.

Accrual-based recording has some potential shortcomings, above and beyond the limitations mentioned above. An often-cited deficiency involves the measurement of accrued tax liabilities so overdue that they can no longer be regarded as collectible because the liable enterprise may already have been liquidated or declared bankrupt. Such overdue taxes or payroll contributions for social security, often subject to unending litigation, cannot reasonably qualify as arrears. The preferred solution on a modified accrual basis is to measure all tax and contribution revenue on a cash basis.

Although cash is the predominant basis of recording worldwide, a number of countries have sought to complement it with, or shift altogether to, a modified

---

[66]Advance tax payments (or other methods of accelerating revenue) have, of course, an effect similar to that of accumulating expenditure arrears, in that they temporarily improve the budget balance under cash-based recording. An analogous case of nontransparency is the recording of extraordinary—though requited—transfers from state-owned enterprises as revenue in the budget, without an offset for the assumption of (e.g., pension) liabilities from those enterprises by the government in an equivalent amount.

[67]A similar practice, found, for example, in Italy and Sri Lanka, involves recording expenditures that have not been incurred because of suspended appropriations. The unused cash is deposited by the spending agencies in government accounts to boost the cash available to meet the public sector borrowing requirement; see Premchand (1994).

[68]See Premchand (1996) for a critique of the problems created for fiscal accounting.

---

[69]According to Teijeiro (1996), this has been an important source of understatement of the officially recorded budget deficit in Argentina in the early 1990s.

[70]Whereas it may be desirable to exclude the inflation component of interest payments for calculating an operational measure of the budget balance (Appendix III), such an adjustment should be executed uniformly, not just for certain indexed securities.

accrual basis, broadly consistent with international accounting standards.[71] So far, only New Zealand has moved to a comprehensive system of accrual-based budgeting, management, and recording; a few others have adopted at least partial accrual recording (e.g., France, Greece, Iceland, Mali, Spain, and Sweden) or intend to move to a full or partial accrual-based approach (e.g., Canada and United Kingdom).[72] More generally, there is increased interest in accrual-based recording, including steps to reconcile existing cash accounts to an accrual basis, partly for greater transparency.[73]

Valuation and Recognition

Accrual-based recording prescribes certain standards for valuation and recognition of assets and liabilities, with implications for the transparency of government financial statements. In this context, the treatment of capital assets and contingent liabilities deserves discussion.

The valuation and recognition of capital assets may be subject to varying treatment depending on the analytical purpose at hand. Accounting fully for investment spending when it is incurred captures the impact on aggregate demand, the focus of macroeconomic stabilization. By contrast, from the standpoint of resource use, only capital depreciation during the period should be shown, regardless of when the acquisition of fixed assets takes place.[74] However, this perspective—in line with the so-called generally accepted accounting practices applicable in the private sector, with full consistency in the calculation of the operat-

ing balance and changes in net worth—is limited for the government because of the difficulty of measuring the depreciation of fixed assets in an economically meaningful way.[75] Indeed, reliable measurement of the value of government assets in infrastructure, given, at best, a rather thin secondary market for such assets, is likely to pose a major difficulty in most countries. Hence, in some cases, it may be necessary to resort to somewhat arbitrary solutions.[76]

In view of the unsolved valuation difficulties—besides the obvious distinction between government and private enterprises, whose objective function is to maximize net worth—the reluctance to prepare full government balance sheets is not surprising. The advanced economies, some developing economies in Asia and Latin America, plus a few economies in transition (Czech Republic, Hungary, and Poland) prepare timely data on gross public debt. Although practically all IMF member countries report data on their official international reserves, only 42 countries report up-to-date information on gross public debt. Most of these countries limit the compilation of government debt to financial obligations serviced through the central budget.[77] (Net government liabilities can then be calculated by deducting financial assets, in the form of securities and foreign assets, from gross debt.) In a few countries (New Zealand and United States), an effort is under way to publish a comprehensive balance sheet for the public sector as a whole. For these and other countries, the measurement of balance sheet information has been influenced by both the generally accepted accounting practices issued by private accounting bodies[78] and by the national accounting standards.[79]

Besides correcting the market value of actual liabilities for inflation, public sector balance sheets are affected by the recognition and valuation of commitments and contingent liabilities. The importance of accumulating such liabilities as a vehicle for spending is underscored when they are substituted for actual government expenditures but not reflected in the fiscal accounts. Most governments undertake commitments (e.g., to multilateral insti-

---

[71]See the revised version in Inter-Secretariat Working Group on National Accounts (1993).

[72]In Australia, several subnational governments employ accrual-based recording, and the Australian National Commission of Audit (1996) has recommended this approach for the national level. In the United States, the Federal Accounting Standards Advisory Board (FASAB) has been responsible for examining government accounting practices and issuing recommendations. For an early recommendation to adopt accrual-based recording, see United States, President's Commission on Budget Concepts (1967).

[73]For example, member countries of the European Union (EU) are required to show their financial statements for the general government on a modified accrual basis for determining compliance with the fiscal criteria under Economic and Monetary Union (EMU); see European Commission (1995). In a recent survey of GFS data users, undertaken by the IMF's Statistics Department, 87 percent of respondents expressed a need for cash-based information, whereas 47 percent indicated that accrual-based data are also required; see Efford (1996).

[74]An advantage of this approach may be apparent in budget-cutting exercises. Under a cash approach, there is an incentive to cut expenditures that will affect the current year's budget, whereas accrual-based recording removes the bias of cutting investment outlays because only the capital used in the year is shown.

[75]See Comiez (1966) for an early discussion of depreciation of government assets, and Coen (1975) for an analysis of economic depreciation in general.

[76]For example, the guidelines issued recently by FASAB have been adopted by the U.S. government.

[77]In some countries, government liabilities are consolidated with those of the central bank, as the latter acts as the government's fiscal agent in external debt management.

[78]At the international level, the Public Sector Committee of the International Federation of Accountants (1996) has proposed guidelines on public sector accounting.

[79]That is, the standards embodied in the System of National Accounts issued by the Inter-Secretariat Working Group on National Accounts (1993), which encompass public sector balance sheets.

tutions) and provide guarantees for credits extended by financial institutions (e.g., for business investment, commodity sales or purchases, and exports) for direct investment overseas and for bank deposits. Often, however, the motive for extending investment or loan guarantees—mainly to industries in difficulty—is the nontransparent postponement of budget outlays. In addition, governments provide social insurance for old age, unemployment, and health care—in most countries, against payroll-based contribution payments.

Although these liabilities represent a potential future obligation for the government, contingent on the realization of the insured occurrence—and thus the need to estimate their unfunded portion—they are not comparable or additive to actual government debt. In general, neither the funded nor the unfunded portions of contingent liabilities relating to social entitlement schemes should be included in the government balance sheet; likewise, changes in such liabilities should not be entered in an accrual-based income statement of the government. However, despite some measurement problems, the actuarial value of net unfunded liabilities for government employees' pensions should normally be included in the calculation of government liabilities in the balance sheet—much like for private enterprises—because they represent a strictly enforceable contractual obligation. This practice, however, is not always followed, even in some major industrial countries. Leaving the arguments for estimating net unfunded government liabilities to Appendix III, it is worth noting here that the measurement of such liabilities is subject to certain technical limitations.[80]

Many countries that compile government debt statistics show separate data on the unfunded portion of contingent liabilities and commitments other than those related to entitlements, specifying the nature of the commitments and contingent liabilities. However, these data are not formally included in a statement of government liabilities outstanding unless they can be quantified and definitely identified as requiring future expenditure. Although most commitments can be quantified, contingent liabilities are more difficult to measure, especially when they are not incurred with the expectation that they will have to be met at some future date. Rather, they are a form of indemnity for the entity receiving the guarantee, which may not be realized. Including the value of such guarantees in the balance sheet requires an assessment of the likelihood of default or some other event likely to require realization of the liability,

which in many cases can be done with acceptable accuracy.[81]

Classification

Fiscal transparency requires that data on government operations be classified into analytically useful categories of flows and stocks. Short of an exhaustive discussion of classification issues, some areas where nontransparency is most prevalent are examined.

First, the breakdown of debt service between interest and amortization payments—and less frequently of certain nontax revenue flows between unrequited transfers and borrowing—is not always available in published government financial statements. Given the indistinguishable nature of such transactions, especially between unrequited transfers and financing, and the ambiguous nature of debt servicing under the former system of central planning, it is still difficult to draw the distinction between "below the line" and "above the line" in a number of countries in transition. There are also some developing countries that traditionally classify certain financing items above the line. An important distortion in measuring fiscal policy, in countries engaged in large-scale privatization of state-owned enterprises, is the inclusion of gross receipts from privatization with other nontax revenue in national presentations.[82]

Second, separation of tax and nontax revenue can be a contentious issue, as is the occasional misclassification of revenue from capital taxation as a form of capital revenue, especially in some economies in transition. Misclassification of revenue by type of tax is rare, except for various types of income taxation, which, at times, is ambiguous. More frequent, however, is the unintended failure to disaggregate revenue at the subnational level of government. Of 83 countries reporting up-to-date revenue data to the

---

[80]For a review of specific technical difficulties encountered in projecting pension obligations, see Van den Noord and Herd (1995) and Franco (1995).

[81]For the United States, for example, in 1997, the government balance sheet contains an assessment of the accrued cost of deposit insurance and private pension scheme guarantees. While known losses on loan guarantees or other contingencies are included in most countries, Italy includes estimates of likely losses on loans, legal claims, and the like. If such estimates cannot be made, some countries (e.g., Netherlands) list contingencies in a separate statement. In New Zealand, for example, all quantifiable and nonquantifiable contingencies are so listed. Quantifiable claims include loans guaranteed for public corporations, callable capital to international and other organizations, prospective costs of contract disputes, and legal claims. Nonquantifiable claims include natural disasters, exchange rate losses incurred by the Reserve Bank of New Zealand, losses incurred as a result of court decisions, and indemnities arising from various regulatory practices. In Canada, the matter is handled through formal provisioning of funds against identified contingent losses likely to be realized.

[82]Under the modified GFS classification, privatization receipts are to be shown below the line to remove the impact of such transactions from the measurement of the thrust of fiscal policy.

IMF, only one-third provided any disaggregation at the subnational level.

Third, deficiencies abound in the classification of government expenditure. Without an adequate breakdown of spending, it is difficult to undertake a meaningful fiscal adjustment plan in terms of the composition of adjustment. Nearly all countries rely primarily on an institutional classification of spending[83] for purposes of budget preparation, legislation, and execution. Only for broad policy planning and analysis do most industrial countries and some developing and transition economies use an economic classification—largely subject to the shortcomings of cash-based accounting. Again, of the countries that reported up-to-date information on government expenditure by economic category, only about one-third did so at the subnational level. Deficiencies in this classification were especially evident in some economies in transition.[84] However, finer distinctions between current and capital outlays tend to be arbitrary even in the most advanced countries, some of which have traditionally failed to separate out capital expenditures in budget statements. Difficulties can also be found in the classification of the wage bill as distinct from other payments for services.

Far more problematic for most countries is to move from an institutional classification to a truly functional disaggregation of outlays. As an example,

although education and cultural spending may be grouped under the same ministry for legislative purposes, these two categories should be shown under separate functions. Relatively few countries are able to approximate satisfactory international standards in this regard, especially at the subnational level. Only 66 countries were able to supply the IMF with such a classification at the central budget or government level, and about 20 countries at the subnational level. Particularly helpful are ongoing reforms in some member countries (e.g., Italy and United Kingdom) to align the management and control of government operations on the basis of a functional classification of expenditures. For analytical purposes, it is useful to separate discretionary spending from expenditure under mandatory programs, insofar as the latter may be altered only through structural reform over the medium to long term.

Finally, disaggregation of financing flows and the corresponding debt stocks by currency denomination, maturity of (securitized) instrument, and source (domestic bank, nonbank, external) is available for only a limited number of countries. Of particular difficulty is establishing consistency between financing flows and the stock of outstanding debt classified on a uniform basis and between financing and revenue and expenditure above the line. Part of the difficulty stems from the diversity of data sources. Whereas below-the-line data on financing are derived mainly from monetary and balance of payments accounts, compiled (for the calendar year) by the central bank or the statistical office, the above-the-line data on government operations are usually recorded (for the fiscal year)—sometimes using a different recording base—by the responsible fiscal authority. Only 40 countries were able to provide timely data on financing flows and corresponding debt stock by type of instrument and creditor at the central government level; of these countries, only a few did so at the subnational level.

---

[83]For an informative critique of the traditional administrative budget in the United States, see United States, President's Commission on Budget Concepts (1967).

[84]The lack of sufficient disaggregation in the *statia* codes, formerly used to compile economic information in the countries of the former Soviet Union, led to a large share of expenditures being lumped into a very large "other expenditure" category; the codes also often failed to distinguish between nonrepayable and repayable payments, that is, between expenditure and net lending, social security contributions, and transfers to various economic sectors. See International Monetary Fund and others (1991) and Montanjees (1995).

Appendix III   Transparency in Indicators and Projections

Building on the discussion of measurement issues, this appendix focuses on the transparency of summary indicators of fiscal policy and performance, as well as of projections of fiscal aggregates. It does not provide an in-depth review or a comparative assessment of fiscal indicators and projections, but examines the transparency of various country practices in this area.

Direct Indicators

The most commonly available fiscal indicator is the overall balance of government operations, published by nearly all IMF member countries on a routine (at least yearly) basis. As a first approximation of the impact of the budget on domestic demand, this indicator is subject to all the distortions in coverage, recording, and classification found in each country's fiscal accounts discussed in Appendix II. Among these distortions, the most prevalent and significant is the exclusion of extrabudgetary operations—particularly social security accounts—and of quasi-fiscal activities. Apart from the above nontransparencies in measurement, some countries present the budget balance by excluding or misclassifying some or all of the economic flows associated with the external sector. Others tend to significantly understate the true deficit and fail to report data on deficit financing. For purposes of policy formulation, certain countries (e.g., Australia and European Union (EU) members) intend to follow the more transparent definition of an "underlying balance," which excludes one-off transactions, especially privatization, even if they otherwise rely on cash-based recording.[85]

Measurement of subsets of the overall balance depends mainly on the adequacy of economic classification, as discussed above. Calculation of the current balance as an indicator of the government's contribution to national saving requires a clear separation of capital and current transactions, which is difficult to achieve without a satisfactory measurement of government investment expenditure. Furthermore, if conventionally measured, government investment may not provide a meaningful gauge of the long-term effect of public spending insofar as it includes some nonproductive capital structures (e.g., executive palaces and monuments) yet excludes current expenditures on human capital through education and health care. Notwithstanding these caveats, many developing countries show separately a capital or development budget balance in the context of their development plans.

Similarly, the primary balance, calculated to determine the fiscal policy effort necessary to stabilize or reduce public debt, requires that net interest payments be excluded from the overall balance. In some countries, interest payments cannot be readily separated from capital transactions or from financing flows. A number of countries (e.g., Argentina, Italy, and United States) include calculations of the primary balance in budget documents. Measurement of the operational balance entails both identification of interest payments and deduction of the corresponding inflationary component of those payments from the overall balance. Notwithstanding some potential measurement problems,[86] the operational balance is routinely calculated, as a supplement to the overall balance, in countries that have experienced high inflation and large domestic indebtedness (e.g., Brazil and Israel). However, some advocates of the operational balance concept argue that even countries with moderate inflation should apply this concept to avoid adopting an inappropriate fiscal policy stance.[87]

---

[85]To determine compliance with the fiscal criteria for participation in European Economic and Monetary Union (EMU), EU members are required to exclude proceeds from privatization—whether undertaken directly or through a state holding company—from government revenue; see European Commission (1995).

[86]As nominal interest rates reflect expected inflation—to compensate the lender for the loss in capital value—the inflationary component should be calculated in reference to the expected rate of inflation rather than the recorded rate of price inflation.

[87]In the United States, during 1977–80, on the basis of an estimate that the real value of net government debt declined by $82 billion, generating a cumulative surplus in that amount (whereas the officially recorded deficits totaled $96 billion, at constant prices), Eisner (1986) argued that the authorities aggravated the ensuing recession by adopting a restrictive monetary and fiscal stance.

Some countries with a traditionally large public enterprise sector (e.g., Italy, Portugal, and United Kingdom) report the public sector borrowing requirement on a cash basis to assess the net impact of the public sector on financial markets, implicitly taking into account the net effect of quasi-fiscal activities of state-owned enterprises and financial institutions, but without revealing the underlying gross flows. Although occasionally subject to debate and to varying treatment, for consistency, privatization receipts are often removed from the public sector borrowing requirement.

Given the difficulties of valuing government assets with precision, gross debt is widely regarded as a more reliable and internationally comparable indicator.[88] Alternatively, by subtracting only negotiable financial assets—mainly domestic securities, gold, and foreign exchange reserves—the net debt ratio could be an acceptable variant.[89] The most ambitious refinement, of course, is the calculation of government net worth. Perhaps because of the ambiguities in valuation and recognition of certain assets and liabilities, only New Zealand has begun to publish a comprehensive and consistent set of statements of the operating budget balance and net worth for the public sector, following the generally accepted accounting practices. (See New Zealand Treasury, 1996.)

Analytical Indicators

Measures of actual government balance and debt, or their variants, as a proportion of GDP may be useful as a first approximation of ex ante fiscal stance and sustainability or of ex post fiscal performance. However, given the inherent limitations of such direct indicators, some countries have adopted a number of more focused analytical indicators, either as a permanent feature or at least on an experimental basis.

To ascertain whether fiscal policy is expansionary, contractionary, or neutral, various summary indicators of fiscal policy stance have been developed by removing the effect of cyclical fluctuations or exogenous shocks from the direct measures of budget balance. The simplest analytical measures of fiscal stance are those based on the full employment surplus (developed in the United States) or the cyclically neutral balance (Germany) and, alter-

natively, of fiscal impulse, measured by the change in the cyclically adjusted effect of the budget (as originally published by the Netherlands). All are compatible with virtually any macroeconomic model and impose rather modest additional data requirements. They require information on the natural rate of unemployment or on a satisfactory measure of the level of potential output. Calculation of the structural balance requires, in addition, estimates of the elasticity of each major tax and transfer category with respect to GDP, which under the cyclically neutral balance are constrained to unity (see Heller, Haas, and Mansur, 1986). Because of the uncertainties surrounding these parameters and estimates of potential output underlying the level of the structural balance, it is preferable to look at the yearly change in the structural balance as indicative of the discretionary thrust of fiscal policy. When the influence of inflation is removed, the operational structural balance provides a useful indicator of discretionary policy in times of inflation. Meanwhile, measures of the primary structural balance abstract the combined influence of interest rates and the debt stock, on the one hand, and of cyclical factors, on the other.

Selection of the appropriate indicator for a given country depends on its stage of development, depth of financial intermediation, tradition, and, perhaps most important, computational convenience. A few governments, or their advisory agencies or councils, publish regularly (Canada, Denmark, Germany, and United States) or occasionally (France) an analytical indicator of fiscal stance, whereas others prefer to calculate such an indicator only for internal purposes.[90] No comparable official calculations can be found in developing countries, because structural shifts preclude reliable time-series estimates of potential output and GDP elasticities of tax revenue or transfer expenditure. Of course, this problem is compounded for economies in transition, where the extraordinary contraction experienced in the first half of the 1990s reflects the radical shift from a centrally planned level of output to a market-determined level of output.

Beyond the short term, it is of much interest to policymakers and financial markets to ascertain whether fiscal policies or, rather, fiscal institutions—including public pension and health care programs—are sustainable well into the future. There are only general definitions of what constitutes sustainable fiscal policy, and economic theory provides little guidance

---

[88]This largely explains the choice of general government gross debt ratio to define the public debt criterion for participation in the EMU.

[89]Along these lines, Canada subtracts all fixed assets valued symbolically at one dollar. Despite widespread agreement about netting out social security reserves, Japan disregards such reserves for precautionary reasons.

[90]In a number of countries, various government agencies may construct their own indicators of fiscal stance. The U.S. Congressional Budget Office calculates the standardized employment deficit. The New Zealand Treasury is experimenting with an "economic fiscal indicator" that allows for a sectoral breakdown.

about the optimal or desirable level and path of the ratio of public debt to GDP.[91] Only the actual prospect of insolvency and debt default signals a clear indication of unsustainability of the public sector. It is, however, useful to determine for any country, even with relatively limited data availability, whether its indebtedness is stable or explosive over the medium term.[92]

A comprehensive indicator of sustainability should include the present value of net unfunded liabilities as a ratio of GDP, particularly liabilities consisting of the future stream of defined benefits for public pension and health care programs, net of existing assets and future contributions to these programs. However, calculating the actuarial value of unfunded liabilities requires long-term projections of social security benefits and contributions, as discussed below. At present, few countries (Canada, United Kingdom, and United States) regularly publish a transparent statement of all actual, as well as funded and unfunded, contingent government liabilities for social entitlement schemes. Recently, the present value of net unfunded public pension liabilities ratio has been calculated for most member countries of the Organization for Economic Cooperation and Development (OECD).[93] The ratio of contingent liabilities to GDP is neither comparable nor additive to the actual debt ratio of the public sector for purposes of determining sustainability. Rather, the ratio of net unfunded government liabilities to GDP should be interpreted as an indicator of the magnitude of the necessary structural reform of the public pension, health care, and other programs—by raising taxes or contributions or by rationalizing benefits—to restore financial viability to the social security system.[94] An

alternative approach to evaluating the necessary adjustment involves calculating the contribution gap.[95]

Whereas the foregoing indicators transparently show whether fiscal policy meets the intertemporal budget constraint, they convey limited information on the intergenerational equity of fiscal benefits and burdens. Increasing concern with not only fiscal sustainability, but also the intergenerational distributional implications, of the existing fiscal structure has spawned the construction of generational accounts, especially in countries with rapidly aging populations. In essence, generational accounts are aimed at calculating the difference between the transfers and services received and the tax payments (in net present value terms and adjusted for productivity growth) of a generation, given the eventual need to satisfy an intertemporal budget constraint.

Notwithstanding some proposals to substitute generational accounts for conventional budget balance measures,[96] the empirical implementation of the former imposes heavy data demands and relies on specific behavioral assumptions derived from the one-good, two-period, life-cycle model. The calculations are highly sensitive to the assumed determination of private savings (with most calculations denying liquidity constraints or a bequest motive); to the selected discount rate and productivity growth; to stylized assumptions about a range of taxes, including those on capital; and to the assumed absence of intergenerational benefit from public consumption or capital spending.

So far, only two countries (Norway and United States) are known to have published official calculations of generational accounts, whereas the OECD has prepared such accounts for five member countries (Germany, Italy, Norway, Sweden, and United States). These calculations suggest that, with unchanged fiscal policies, generations born in the mid-1990s can expect to face significantly higher tax burdens than present generations in most of these countries.[97] Although, clearly, it would be difficult to

---

[91]For example, according to a general definition in Bean and Buiter (1987, p. 27), "a government is solvent if its spending programme, its tax-transfer programme, and its planned future use of seigniorage [that is, its ability to issue currency at a face value in excess of its cost of production] are consistent with its outstanding, initial financial and real assets and liabilities (in the sense that the present value of its spending programme is equal to its comprehensive net worth)." For a theoretical treatment of sustainability, see Horne (1991). See also proposals by Parker and Kastner (1993) for a practical framework for assessing fiscal sustainability in IMF-supported programs.

[92]The stability condition is given by the equation $\Delta d = [(r-g)/(1+g)]d_{-1} - pb$, where d is the debt-to-GDP ratio, pb is the ratio of the primary balance to GDP, r is the nominal interest rate on public debt, and g is the growth rate of nominal GDP. See, for example, the calculations for major industrial countries in International Monetary Fund (1996b, pp. 50–51).

[93]For 10 OECD member countries, the estimated present value of net unfunded pension liabilities reaches or exceeds the level of GDP, assuming a 5 percent discount rate and 1.5 percent yearly productivity growth. See Roseveare and others (1996) and Organization for Economic Cooperation and Development (1996a, pp. 36–37).

[94]To illustrate the point, in the United States, as a result of the 1983 amendments to the Social Security Act, the present value of net unfunded liabilities of the old-age, survivors', disability, and

hospital insurance programs fell from 70 percent of GNP at end-1982 to less than 10 percent by end-1983.

[95]The contribution gap is the difference between a constant sustainable contribution rate that, over a long time, would lead to no buildup of pension debt above an initial level and the expected average contribution rate under existing budget law. See, for example, Chand and Jaeger (1996).

[96]For an overview of generational accounts, see Auerbach, Gokhale, and Kotlikoff (1994), and for a critical assessment, see Haveman (1994).

[97]See United States, Office of Management and Budget (1995), Hagemann and John (1995), and Organization for Economic Cooperation and Development (1995b). Italy shows the most inequitable outcome; there, future generations will have to pay five times larger net taxes than the present generation, assuming a 5 percent discount rate and 1.5 percent yearly productivity growth.

prepare such estimates over a wide range of countries, private researchers have attempted similar calculations for a number of other industrial countries (Australia, Denmark, New Zealand, and United Kingdom). As with the estimates of unfunded liabilities, generational accounts should be regarded merely as a broad indicator of the structural adjustment required to avoid aggravating the inequities among generations.

Projections

The formulation of fiscal policy as well as the concomitant public debate are usually predicated on projections of future trends in government finances and in overall economic performance. The more transparent the projections, the more informed the public debate and the more credible and sustainable the resulting fiscal policy decisions. Broadly speaking, explicit, realistic, timely, and internally consistent projections—whether model-based or judgmental—can be regarded as transparent. But transparency in the underlying macroeconomic projections does not necessarily ensure transparent fiscal projections. Transparency needs to be examined separately under different time frames: short- to medium-term forecasts, as distinct from long-term scenarios.

Short- to Medium-Term Forecasts

With the exception of the economies in transition and the least developed market economies, most IMF member countries have come a long way in developing and improving their ability to prepare macroeconomic forecasts through some combination of econometric or computational models and judgment.[98] The resulting macroeconomic forecasts provide the framework for forecasting fiscal aggregates. Although virtually all governments disclose forecasts of key macroeconomic indicators (growth, inflation, unemployment, interest rates, and key commodity prices), they may be reluctant to reveal the methods they use to derive them, including behavioral and technological parameters.[99] However, most advanced economies and some developing economies disclose the detailed macroeconomic forecasts they use as the basis of fiscal forecasting.[100]

In the past, governments often adopted assumptions that were difficult to justify, especially about interest rates, unemployment rates, and output and income growth, so as to understate government expenditure forecasts and overstate revenue forecasts. The propensity for such practices—often based on assertions rather than on transparent measurement using empirical relationships—was particularly high when governments felt compelled to meet short- or medium-term fiscal targets. In recent years, however, many countries have become more realistic, open, and consistent in their forecasts, realizing that they are likely to be evaluated and challenged by their legislatures, the public, and financial markets. Under one approach (e.g., Canada), the government relies on consensual macroeconomic forecasts for the preparation of fiscal projections.[101] Following another approach, country authorities deliberately use conservative macroeconomic assumptions (e.g., Chile and Netherlands).[102] In a number of countries (e.g., Austria, Germany, Sweden, and United Kingdom), transparency has been enhanced by open debate with independent forecasting agencies or panels, created to assist governments in selecting realistic forecast values.

In preparing fiscal forecasts and the accompanying macroeconomic forecasts, policymakers should provide, separately, baseline projections that assume unchanged policies and alternative projections incorporating the impact of major (anticipated or recommended) policy changes. In most countries, official projections usually include policy measures, with the net budgetary impact of the measures—in terms of the value of revenue and expenditure measures—shown separately. Under the circumstances, the scope for nontransparent practices is rather ample. For example, poorly documented, pessimistic baseline projections may give a misleading impression of the size

---

[98]A government has the prerogative to choose the most appropriate framework—emphasizing, for example, Keynesian, Ricardian, or various eclectic features—and to supplement model-based results with judgment as to elements—particularly, credibility effects—that are not always captured satisfactorily by those results. Alternatively, lacking adequate data or statistically significant estimates, it may justifiably decide to rely purely on computational or judgmental methods. Transparency simply requires explicit and timely disclosure and, preferably, the publication of methods to permit public assessment of the quality, including consistency, and track record of the forecasts.

[99]In Australia, Sweden, and the United Kingdom, for example, the macroeconomic model used for official fiscal forecasting is available to the public.

[100]Although they still face severe data constraints, a number of transition economies are also pushing ahead with developing their macroeconomic forecasting capability.

[101]Canada's Department of Finance adopts assumptions on the basis of an average of forecasts prepared by private institutions, with a prudential margin added to interest rates. The impact of these upward-adjusted rates is reflected in output and inflation assumptions, with the private sector averages being revised accordingly. Thus, for example, the short-term interest rate assumption for fiscal year 1997/98 was raised by 80 basis points above the private sector consensus.

[102]In France, for example, the budget deficit for 2001 was initially based on a 2.1 percent annual medium-term GDP growth rate—at the time seen as a conservative assumption—to signal adherence to the target even under less favorable cyclical conditions. In Chile, for the macroeconomic and budget forecasts, a relatively low price is assumed for copper exports.

of the required fiscal adjustment.[103] A less obvious distortion involves reliance on rather opaque implicit tax or expenditure parameters. Instead, a fully documented set of baseline and policy projections, including feedback effects, should be published.[104]

Preparation of comprehensive forecasts is, of course, beyond the reach of many nonindustrial countries, particularly economies in transition that are undergoing rapid structural change and lack adequate databases. In the interest of transparency, these countries should offer a public explanation of even rudimentary forecasting methods and assumptions used, so that users can gain some perception of the risks—both upside and downside—inherent in the forecasts. Although a significant number of member countries possess a modest forecasting capacity, the authorities seldom publish a note explaining the forecasts.

Quite apart from a rather uneven disclosure of the methodology and basic assumptions, nearly all IMF member governments provide fairly detailed forecasts for the annual central budget, subject to deficiencies in classification (Appendix II), as part of the draft budget bill they submit for legislative enactment for the upcoming fiscal year. Particularly enlightening for users of fiscal forecasts—lacking sufficient information on methods—is the publication of (1) a sensitivity analysis showing the response of fiscal aggregates to a marginal change in key macroeconomic variables, (2) a breakdown between discretionary and mandatory spending, and (3) supporting forecasts of "cost drivers," such as the number of government employees and the number of beneficiaries of entitlements (e.g., Australia, Canada, and United States).

Detailed and open documentation of microeconomic linkages and assumptions (e.g., effective tax rates, tax bases, and parameters, including compliance coefficients or collection lags, used for each revenue category) underlying the fiscal forecasts is not readily available in most countries. As a result, it is difficult to assess any deviations of outcome from forecasts for specific revenue or expenditure categories.[105] Yet, logically, initial budget forecasts

should be followed with periodic updates and an evaluation of how outcomes deviate from forecasts. In fact, several OECD member countries (Australia, New Zealand, United Kingdom, and United States) publish within-year updates, even in the absence of supplementary budget legislation. Such updates should be accompanied, if possible, by a public explanation of the reasons for significant deviations from forecasts.[106]

With increasing concern for sustainability, in the 1980s, some industrial countries (Italy, Netherlands, Sweden, and United States) began developing multiyear budget projections—often contrasted with baseline projections—in the context of medium-term fiscal consolidation plans. At present, in some countries, these forecasts are simply meant to provide top-down guidance on the need for discretionary fiscal action beyond the current one-year budget period, that is, the baseline for formulating medium-term budget priorities. In some countries (France and Japan), the multiyear projections provide the context for the medium-term outlook for only the broadest fiscal aggregates, without necessarily spelling out the actual policy measures to be used for attaining the fiscal target.[107] Nevertheless, a number of countries (Australia, Germany, Italy, Netherlands, New Zealand, Switzerland, United Kingdom, and United States) provide detailed medium-term fiscal forecasts incorporating the authorities' policy intentions.[108] Regardless of the approach used, the message of such exercises is that the built-in momentum of existing programs—especially mandatory entitlement programs—measured against the revenue yield of

---

[103]In Italy, for example, the baseline budget was occasionally inflated because spending ministries were asked to calculate the cost of maintaining existing policies with no regard for potential cost savings.

[104]In the United States, both the Office of Management and Budget, which is responsible for forecasts incorporating all policy proposals of the administration, and the Congressional Budget Office, directly responsible to the Congress, prepare separate projections of baseline "current services" and of the effect of new policy measures. Differences between the two sets of projections reflect primarily differences in economic and technical assumptions.

[105]This is illustrated, for example, by the significant unanticipated shortfall in the value-added tax and corporate income tax revenue recorded recently in the United Kingdom.

---

[106]In Australia, for example, the authorities provided the following summary reconciliation for fiscal year 1995/96 (in billions of Australian dollars):

Revenue forecast	124.4
Effect of policy changes	–0.2
Effect of adjustment in parameters and other changes	–2.5
Revenue outcome	121.7
Expenditure forecast	123.7
Effect of policy changes	0.8
Effect of wage and price adjustments	0.4
Effect of adjustment in parameters	0.2
Other adjustments	1.7
Expenditure outcome	126.7

Source: Statement 1 to *Budget Speech 1996/97* (Australia, Department of the Treasury, 1997).

[107]In Japan, the Ministry of Finance has prepared both baseline and policy-adjusted projections covering the period through 2006; see Okamura (1996).

[108]In several countries (e.g., Germany, New Zealand, and Switzerland), these forecasts are limited to the central government.

existing tax policies leaves a narrow, if any, margin for new program initiatives.[109]

Long-Run Scenarios

A growing concern with long-term financial sustainability in view of rapidly aging populations, the rising cost of health care, and the rigidity of most social entitlements prompted some governments in industrial countries to prepare long-term scenarios showing the annual fiscal balance over a period of up to seven decades. They have carried out these calculations, mostly on an occasional basis, to examine the sustainability of existing public pension systems.[110] There are, however, a few countries where social security agencies are legally required to publish each year long-term projections separately for each retirement fund (Canada and United States) and each health care fund (United States)[111] under alternative sets of general assumptions regarding economic growth, wage growth, interest rates, inflation, unemployment, fertility, net migration, and mortality, as well as under specific assumptions about disability, hospital, and medical costs. On the basis of these baseline projections, it is possible to test the effect of alternative reform op-

tions, such as tightening eligibility criteria for specific pension benefits or various cost-containment measures in health care programs.[112]

Overall, these scenarios contain considerable information, particularly regarding the path of financial balance over a prolonged period, and can be used to simulate in a transparent manner the effect of corrective reform measures.[113] Furthermore, these scenario results can be summarized, using the present value of net unfunded government liabilities to choose an appropriate discount rate, as discussed above. Expressed as a percentage of GDP, the former can be interpreted as an indicator of fiscal sustainability, comparable across countries and over time. In view of the acknowledged uncertainties about the underlying macroeconomic and demographic projections and assumptions, presentation of scenario results should always be accompanied by a sensitivity test with respect to changes in key assumptions.

---

[109]In the United Kingdom, this process was for a time strengthened by a new emphasis on imposition of cash limits on many budget aggregates—a warning to managers that initial estimates had to be prepared more carefully and that the source of potential error, including the interaction of cost factors with prospective macroeconomic forecasts, had to be carefully reconciled. Although in the United States the projections are highly disaggregated for mandatory and discretionary programs, projections of discretionary expenditures depend on yearly appropriations and cannot be made effective through current legislative actions.

[110]See the review of national projections for EU member countries in Franco and Munzi (1996).

[111]In the United States, this requirement encompasses moving 10-year and 75-year projections separately for the old-age and survivors' insurance, disability insurance, and hospital insurance trust funds. For the 10-year projection, the trust fund ratio (trust fund reserves as a percentage of annual benefit payments) is calculated; the 75-year projection consists of a summary actuarial

balance (annual revenue less payments as a ratio of taxable payroll, adjusted to include the beginning fund reserves and the cost of ending the projection period with reserves equivalent to yearly benefit payments). The purpose of the exercise is to ascertain the profile of these indicators over time and to determine the period until exhaustion of the reserves in each fund. As of end-1995, the remaining period under intermediate assumptions was 35 years for the old-age and survivors' insurance, 19 years for disability insurance, and 5 years for hospital insurance; see Social Security and Medicare Boards of Trustees (1995). Canada also prepares detailed long-run projections for public pension programs; see Canadian Pension Plan Secretariat (1996).

[112]See, for example, the recent long-term simulations, incorporating hypothetical reform options for the old-age and survivors' insurance and the hospital insurance programs, in United States, Congressional Budget Office (1996).

[113]Ideally, of course, policy simulations should be performed with an appropriate economywide model that allows fully for endogenous macroeconomic repercussions of the hypothesized policy changes. See, for instance, the application of such a model in the United States in Aaron, Bosworth, and Burtless (1989). The most recent set of model-based policy scenarios can be found in United States, Congressional Budget Office (1996).

Appendix IV Selected Country Experiences

This appendix summarizes the experiences of selected countries in several regions of the IMF's membership. Although none of the countries selected is necessarily to be regarded as a model of fiscal transparency, each has made significant progress toward transparency within its own region in recent years. The impetus for improvement came largely from within, in some cases with support from the IMF.

Botswana

Within Africa, Botswana has achieved a substantial degree of fiscal transparency. Factors that have contributed to transparency include a prudent and open budget process and a high level of competence in the civil service.

The government's fiscal policy strategy is set down in published five-year development plans. However, these plans are revised periodically to take into account the evolving economic situation. Thus, in the published midterm review of the current plan, expected revenue shortfalls were identified, along with intended measures to reduce current expenditure and improve project implementation. Successive budget surpluses, driven by strong growth in mining revenues, contributed to a large accumulation of government deposits with the banking system and associated foreign exchange reserves.

The Seventh Development Plan, covering the period 1991/92 to 1996/97, announced publicly that the country intended to run down cash deposits to fund a revenue shortfall as mineral revenues slowed and current expenditures increased. During the preparation of the Eighth Development Plan, the Ministry of Finance and Planning released to the public a policy paper setting down the thrust of fiscal policies over the period to 2002/2003. Given the anticipated slowdown in revenues, particularly from the mining sector, the paper prudently highlighted the options to curtail the growth of government expenditure.

Tax legislation clearly specifies the rates and taxable bases. The authorities have resisted pressure to expand the extensive investment and other concessions available under the tax system. Tax administra-
tors have limited discretion, and appeals are possible. At this time, the main problem in tax administration is the buildup of tax arrears, on which only limited information is available.

Operations of the central budget are recorded on a cash basis, with a clear breakdown of tax and nontax revenues and a functional and economic classification of expenditures, which accord with international standards. Although no balance sheet is prepared, accurate up-to-date records of gross internal and external government debt are published. Detailed annual data on the central budget are normally published with a lag of two to three months. Nonfinancial public enterprises and public financial institutions are required to publish annual reports. No comprehensive data on local government operations are available.

Although Botswana has an extensive range of financial and nonfinancial public enterprises, the authorities have largely avoided using these enterprises to engage in quasi-fiscal activities.

Chile

In the mid-1970s, Chile formulated an economic strategy to facilitate private sector development by reducing the size and role of government. It has maintained this strategy over time, and the scope of government activities has shrunk significantly. Subsequently, priority has shifted to improving efficiency in government activities, to ensuring that fiscal management is consistent with broader macroeconomic and social objectives, and to enhancing the overall transparency of public finances.

The role of the government has been reshaped through privatization of state-owned enterprises; decentralization of government activities (e.g., in primary and secondary education); shifting of traditional government services to the private sector (including health care insurance and management of pension funds); increasing of private sector ownership or participation in the construction, operation, and maintenance of public infrastructure (including electricity generation and distribution, harbors, and transport projects); and effective operation of the copper fund.

The government budget has been in surplus over the last decade, partly as a result of these reforms.

The budget process has been designed to achieve transparent control over public finances and to ensure consistency of fiscal policy with the announced macroeconomic objectives. Each year, the draft budget submitted to the legislature contains policy statements on macroeconomic targets, supported by relatively conservative assumptions for key macro variables (including the export price of copper). It includes detailed operating plans for each spending agency and detailed revenue estimates by tax category. The draft budget is subject to review by specialized legislative committees; since 1995, budget execution has been monitored on the basis of quarterly statements submitted by the Budget Office of the Ministry of Finance with a lag of 60–90 days. The quarterly reports are widely available through publications and the electronic media (Internet).

Although operated outside the budget, the copper stabilization fund has played an important role in the budget process since its creation in 1981. The fund is required to deposit the revenues that exceed an established benchmark in a special account at the central bank. Use of the fund was initially restricted to debt service and subsequently to prepayment of public debt. In 1986, legislation formally establishing the Copper Compensation Fund provided clear rules for deposits and withdrawals on the basis of the difference between a medium-term reference price and the actual export price of copper. Changes in operating procedures for this fund must be jointly agreed to by four institutions: the central bank, CODELCO (the state-owned copper corporation), the treasury, and the budget office. Prudent management of the Copper Compensation Fund under transparent rules has lessened the impact of external shocks and allowed for a buildup of foreign exchange reserves. However, less transparent is the allocation of 10 percent of gross copper exports by CODELCO—equivalent to 0.6 percent of GDP during the 1990s—for military expenditures to a fund operating outside the budget. This allocation is in addition to the regular budgetary allocations to the Ministry of Defense.

Tax reform has resulted in a simple system, by international standards, with comparatively low rates and transparent bases. Tax administration has become broadly transparent, although some past exemptions have been grandfathered under various statutes, making it difficult to assess their full implications; also, these exemptions follow a variety of less than clearly defined objectives. The authorities have yet to develop a tax expenditure budget.

Reports on budgetary accounts, recorded on a cash basis, include consolidated central government operations and the operations of state-owned enterprises, but exclude those of the local governments.

Government expenditures are classified by economic, functional, and institutional categories, and revenues are classified by tax categories, consistent with international standards. Chile subscribes to the IMF's Special Data Dissemination Standard.

For a limited number of decentralized agencies (such as institutions of higher education), only budgetary transfers are recorded, whereas for the public financial institutions, comprehensive reports are published on a regular basis. The central bank's balance sheet contains aggregate data on quasi-fiscal operations associated with schemes to support the banking system during the crisis of the early 1980s and with the placement of promissory notes for sterilization purposes. State-owned enterprises are operated transparently without hidden subsidies or preferential credits.

As part of the process of increasing the efficiency and transparency of government operations, the authorities are developing selective performance indicators for spending agencies. Recently, they adopted a pilot project and are expanding it to 65 specialized agencies by 1997, covering areas such as public works, mining, education, health care, and finance.

Denmark

Significant efforts have been made to improve the transparency of government operations in Denmark to strengthen financial discipline and to enhance oversight by the electorate. The driving force for these reforms has been the large size of the general government (total expenditures amount to 60 percent of GDP) and the high degree of decentralization (more than half of government expenditures are at the subnational level). The reforms included major legislative changes and deregulation in various areas, including financial and labor markets.

One of the key measures enhancing fiscal transparency was the harmonization of the budgetary systems of the central and local governments, which facilitated the publication of the annual consolidated general government budget. This entailed prescribing common budget standards, adopting a meaningful system of classification, and laying down a strict timetable for the preparation and legislative approval of the budgets at all levels. Current legislative provisions require all governments to disseminate clear information on their operations (in the form of pamphlets) prior to the budget debates in the national and subnational legislatures.

The government budget has been transformed from a mere accounting and monitoring device to an information vehicle to assist political decision making. The introduction of compulsory multiyear budgeting at all government levels has strengthened the budget as an instrument for medium-term policy planning by shifting the emphasis from short-term fiscal management to setting strategic priorities and longer-term objectives. Its introduction has been underpinned by comprehensive analyses of consolidated multiyear public investment programs for all levels of government. Government operations are now reviewed regularly by specialized bodies of fiscal audit, which publish their findings to further increase the accountability of government entities. The central and local governments are also required to monitor budgetary developments closely during the budget year and to prepare supplementary budgets if necessary.

In recent years, considerable efforts have been made to simplify the tax system. As a result, a large number of personal income tax payers need not file tax returns; tax authorities rely instead on administrative records for information on incomes, which are sent to taxpayers for verification. A system of advance rulings has been introduced to facilitate taxpayer awareness of compliance requirements, while a comprehensive statute protects taxpayers from discretionary action.

Denmark subscribes to the Special Data Dissemination Standard. The fiscal accounts, prepared annually, have a broad coverage that extends to the consolidated general government. This presentation typically forms the basis for the budget process and the determination of intergovernmental fiscal transfers for the forthcoming year (e.g., grants for new tasks to be performed at the subnational level). Although the accounts follow a cash-based recording, this approach has been supplemented in recent years by accrual-based recording for some items. The classification of expenditures and revenues closely follows international standards. Although no balance sheets are published, aggregate information on the value of public sector assets and liabilities (including a detailed breakdown of gross central government debt) is published on a regular basis.

Denmark regularly publishes official estimates of the fiscal impulse and the structural deficit for the general government sector, which the Ministry of Finance updates at least four times a year. Quasi-fiscal activities are virtually nonexistent. There has been considerable privatization; the public enterprises that remain are required to meet commercial criteria.

Hungary

Hungary has evolved from a country with secretive and nontransparent fiscal practices—including misreporting to the IMF—under socialist central planning to the one with probably the highest level of transparency among economies in transition as it becomes an emerging financial market. This transformation has been assisted by an active legislative and institution-building process. However, like other economies in transition, Hungary has yet to reach a level comparable to that of most industrial countries.

Since the early 1990s, Hungary has operated a highly decentralized and complex budget system, with the central budget receiving the revenue from the major tax categories and then making transfers to autonomous central budgetary institutions, extrabudgetary funds, and local governments. Although the Ministry of Finance exercised overall control over budget transfers, the system conferred considerable freedom of action on the various participants, many of whom retained some own-source revenue (mainly user fees) and were not subject to detailed monitoring of expenditure. The implementation of a centralized treasury system in 1996—with a single bank account through which all central budget revenues and expenditures are effected under the scrutiny of the Ministry of Finance—has contributed to both improved central budget control and transparency. However, the social security funds retain considerable independence, and reporting deficiencies make monitoring the funds' activities difficult.

Timely data on general government operations are not yet available. For operational purposes, the authorities rely on information on the consolidated central government, which encompasses the central budget (including the operations of the central budgetary institutions partly financed by own revenues) and extrabudgetary funds (including social security funds). Data on over 3,000 subnational governments are available only with a significant time lag. Although subject to legislative approval, the operations of the privatization agency are excluded from the coverage of the consolidated central government (e.g., as in Germany). In 1996, the bulk of privatization receipts were earmarked in a transparent manner for debt reduction, although some allocations (partly in the form of loan guarantees) were made directly to state-owned enterprises (notably, the Borsod steel complex) and local governments.

Although all transactions are recorded on a cash basis, up-to-date information is made available for social security contribution arrears and contingent liabilities. Institutional and economic classification of expenditures is published for the consolidated central government, and a comprehensive functional classification is under development within the recently formed treasury.

Considerable progress has been made in compiling comprehensive data on financing flows for the consolidated central government, largely from balance sheet information prepared by the National Bank of Hungary. Indeed, gross debt data for the consolidated central government are published annually. Until recently, the task of compiling such information had been complicated by the unique public sector debt-management arrangements, whereby the National Bank of Hungary acted as the sovereign borrower abroad while the Ministry of Finance managed domestic debt. This arrangement was discontinued in 1997, and the Ministry of Finance assumed responsibility for managing all government debt and publishing comprehensive data on government liabilities. Information on new guaranteed debt to nonfinancial public enterprises is now published in the budget each year.

Like all former centrally planned economies, in the past, Hungary conducted a large number of quasi-fiscal activities through state-owned enterprises and financial institutions, although not to the extent of some of its neighbor countries, and the ongoing reforms and large-scale privatization have reduced the extent of quasi-fiscal activities still further. Although some nontransparent subsidies remain, the authorities have replaced most with explicit transfers from the budget. A legacy in this area is the large nonperforming loans—mainly to bankrupt state-owned enterprises—held by several state-owned banks. By 1995, the issuance of government paper to finance capital injections to these banks had been completed, with the servicing of the debt subsequently assumed by, and shown transparently in, the central budget. The remaining tasks of rationalization (including debt workouts and downsizing of a redundant workforce) and privatization are under way.

Although all the major taxes have been codified in tax laws—Hungary was the first former centrally planned economy to introduce fairly transparent tax rates and bases in the late 1980s—some remain excessively complex and are impaired by frequent regulatory changes. During the transition, a number of largely ad hoc exemptions and deductions were granted to private, especially foreign-owned, companies. Although the effect of past arrangements still persists, the ad hoc granting of new tax concessions was discontinued in 1994. The budget documents provide only fragmentary information on tax expenditures.

The State Audit Office, established in 1992, is fulfilling a mandate to prepare and publish reports on the performance of budgetary institutions, social security agencies, and selected state-owned enterprises.

Jordan

In recent years, Jordan has made substantial progress toward transparency. Historically, Jordan did not formulate a fiscal strategy. The need for a more concerted approach to fiscal restraint was clearly underscored by the explosion of government deficits and debt in the late 1980s. Since then, Jordan has publicly announced a medium-term fiscal strategy, supported by an Extended Arrangement with the IMF.

The budget law is enacted by the end of each year in accordance with comprehensive arrangements for the conduct of fiscal policy: the Ministry of Finance has the primary responsibility for preparing and executing the budget. The draft budget is reviewed by a parliamentary finance committee before it is submitted for legislative action.

Comprehensive information is available monthly and annually for the central government budget, which covers all departments and the Jordan Valley Authority. Budget coverage has improved substantially since 1990; it now includes within its ambit all extrabudgetary operations, except defense. A portion of defense spending is handled through an extrabudgetary fund that is financed through foreign loans. Military wages and operating costs are on-budget, but from published data it is difficult to determine the split between the two components. Earmarked revenues (in particular, a portion of import duties) are channeled directly to municipalities and universities and do not appear in the budget. Limited information is available on a number of decentralized government agencies (such as universities, institutes, marketing authorities, and other agencies) that, besides their own revenue sources, are also supported to varying degrees by budget transfers and state-owned financial and nonfinancial entities.

Government accounts are recorded on a cash basis and published with a two-month lag. The classification used in the annual budget follows a largely institutional format, but the authorities compile data for the Fund's *Government Finance Statistics Yearbook,* reclassifying revenues, expenditures (both by functional and by economic type), and financing transactions according to international standards. Comprehensive data are also compiled on both external and internal gross public debt. Although no separate information is available on the large and accumulating unfunded liabilities of the public pension system, data on loan guarantees are published by the Central Bank of Jordan.

Jordan has a large state-owned enterprise sector, and the government owns shares in some private enterprises through its holding company, the Jordan Investment Corporation. Although these enterprises can borrow domestically, guarantees must be approved by the legislature. Overall, it is difficult to assess the relationship between the enterprises and the government. An annual report on public enterprises includes a consolidated balance sheet; however, no information is available on the extent of their quasi-fiscal activities. To improve the monitoring of public finances and increase transparency, public enterprises will be required to submit monthly financial statements and quarterly projections of revenue and expenditure to the Ministry of Finance.

The tax system has been simplified and modernized. The principal objective of the reforms has been to lower marginal rates, reduce the number of rates, and broaden tax bases. In principle, the degree of discretion in tax administration has been reduced. Tariff rates have been reduced and unified and customs procedures simplified. However, multiple rates and extensive exemptions and deductions remain, and the determination of tax liabilities is still often subject to considerable negotiation and administrative interpretation. Taxpayer rights and responsibilities are clearly specified.

New Zealand

New Zealand represents a benchmark for public sector transparency. The Fiscal Responsibility Act of 1994, which contains a set of principles for fiscal management and transparency, is the culmination of a decade of reform designed to improve the efficiency, effectiveness, and accountability of what had been a large and interventionist public sector.[114] Until the mid-1980s, economic performance in New Zealand was disappointing because of inadequate adjustment to changes in the world economy. Since then, the government has made solid progress in downsizing the public sector, moving the budget into surplus, and reducing public debt. The measures to increase fiscal transparency may be seen partly as a means of assuring domestic and overseas investors that the government, regardless of political orientation, is committed to behaving responsibly.

The government is required to follow the fiscal management principles established in the Fiscal Responsibility Act, whose goals consist in reducing and maintaining debt at prudent levels; aiming for a balanced operating budget within a reasonable time frame, with allowance for cyclically induced deficits or surpluses; providing a buffer against possible adverse developments by maintaining adequate levels of net worth in the government balance sheet; and ensuring a reasonable degree of predictability about the level and stability of taxes. (The government is allowed to depart temporarily from these principles provided it explains its reasons and indicates how, and within what time frame, it plans to return to them.) In addition, the legislation obliges the government to publish the following: a budget policy statement setting down its strategic priorities for the coming fiscal year as well as its long-term objectives regarding revenue, expenditure, deficit and debt levels, and net worth; an economic and fiscal update containing economic and fiscal forecasts for the current budget year and the following two fiscal years; and a fiscal strategy report that explains whether the update is consistent with the government's previously stated intentions and that projects the path of all relevant fiscal variables for at least 10 years. A separate preelection economic and fiscal update must be published two to six weeks before an election. The government is required to disclose all items involving fiscal costs or gains and to identify potential risks.[115]

The tax system is simple and contains clearly specified tax rates and bases. The Inland Revenue Department has limited administrative discretion in the application of the tax laws. The department assists taxpayers by publishing technical information on specific points of interpretation. Since 1992, the department can also issue legally binding rulings. Estimates of tax expenditures are not published—the substantial curtailment of tax deductions and concessions has rendered this task unnecessary. The law specifies taxpayer rights and obligations.

Public accounts are reported on a whole-of-government basis, which covers the consolidated central government (including decentralized entities) as well as nonfinancial public enterprises and public financial institutions (including the central bank). Subnational governments are not included in these accounts, but information on this relatively small sector is now collected in a timely fashion by the statistical agency. Quasi-fiscal activities are not separately identified, but their net impact is implicitly captured in the whole-of-government data. New Zealand's accounting statements are accrual-based, but cash accounts continue to be published. Scope for creative accounting is constrained by the requirement to conform to standards set by the independent Accounting Standards Review Board. Detailed classifications of revenues and expenditures follow international standards. Comprehensive national balance sheets are produced semiannually. The statements attached to the balance sheets explain revaluation changes and contain comprehensive listings and estimates (where quantifiable) of all measurable commitments and contingent liabilities.

---

[114]For a more complete account of these reforms, see Cangiano (1996) and Scott (1996).

[115]The Fiscal Responsibility Act requires that all government financial statements (including projections) be drawn up in accordance with generally accepted accounting practices and thus meet the same standards (set by the Accounting Standards Review Board) as private sector financial reports. The Minister of Finance must formally accept overall responsibility for the integrity of the disclosures and their consistency with the act, and must also state that all relevant information has been transmitted to the Secretary of the Treasury.

References

Aaron, Henry J., Barry P. Bosworth, and Gary T. Burt-less, 1989, *Can America Afford to Grow Old? Paying for Social Security* (Washington: Brookings Institution).

Alesina, Alberto, and Alex Cukierman, 1990, "The Politics of Ambiguity," *Quarterly Journal of Economics*, Vol. 105 (November), pp. 829–50.

Alesina, Alberto, and others, 1995, "Budget Institutions and Fiscal Performance in Latin America," IDB Working Paper WP-004 (Washington: Inter-American Development Bank, Office of the Chief Economist).

Alexander, William E., and others, 1997, *Systemic Bank Restructuring and Macroeconomic Policy* (Washington: International Monetary Fund).

Auerbach, Alan J., Jagadeesh Gokhale, and Laurence J. Kotlikoff, 1994, "Generational Accounting: A Meaningful Way to Evaluate Fiscal Policy," *Journal of Economic Perspectives*, Vol. 8 (Winter), pp. 73–94.

Australia, National Commission of Audit, 1996, *Report to the Commonwealth Government* (Canberra: Australian Government Publishing Service).

———, Department of the Treasury, 1997, *Budget Speech 1996/97* (Canberra).

Bean, Charles R., and Willem H. Buiter, 1987, *The Plain Man's Guide to Fiscal and Financial Policy* (London: Employment Institute).

Blejer, Mario I., and Adrienne Cheasty, eds., 1993, *How to Measure the Fiscal Deficit: Analytical and Methodological Issues* (Washington: International Monetary Fund).

Buchanan, James M., and Richard E. Wagner, 1977, *Democracy in Deficit: The Political Legacy of Lord Keynes* (New York: Academic Press).

Canada, Canadian Pension Plan Secretariat, 1996, "An Information Paper for Consultations on the Canadian Pension Plan," condensed version, released by the Federal, Provincial, and Territorial Governments of Canada (Ottawa: Department of Finance).

Cangiano, Marco, 1996, "Accountability and Transparency in the Public Sector: The New Zealand Experience," IMF Working Paper 96/122 (Washington: International Monetary Fund).

Chand, Sheetal K., and Albert Jaeger, 1996, *Aging Populations and Public Pension Schemes*, IMF Occasional Paper No. 147 (Washington: International Monetary Fund).

Coen, Robert M., 1975, "Investment Behavior, the Measurement of Depreciation, and Tax Policy," *American Economic Review*, Vol. 65 (March), pp. 59–74.

Comiez, Maynard S., 1966, *A Capital Budget Statement for the U.S. Government* (Washington: Brookings Institution).

Efford, Don, 1996, "The Case for Accrual Recording in the IMF's Government Finance Statistics System," IMF Working Paper 96/73 (Washington: International Monetary Fund).

Eisner, Robert, 1986, *How Real Is the Federal Deficit?* (New York: Free Press).

European Commission, 1995, "Methodological and Operational Aspects of the Reporting of Government Deficits and Debt Levels in the Context of the Excessive Deficit Procedure" (Brussels: Directorate General II).

Franco, Daniele, 1995, "Pension Liabilities: Their Use and Misuse in the Assessment of Fiscal Policies," European Commission Economic Papers No. 110 (Brussels: Directorate-General for Economic and Financial Affairs).

———, and Teresa Munzi, 1996, "Public Pension Expenditure Prospects in the European Union: A Survey of National Projections," in *Ageing and Pension Expenditure Prospects in the Western World*, European Economy, Reports and Studies, No. 3 (Luxembourg: European Commission, Directorate-General for Economic and Financial Affairs).

Gansler, Jacques S., 1995, *Defense Conversion: Transforming the Arsenal of Democracy* (Cambridge: MIT Press).

Gore, Albert, 1993, *From Red Tape to Results: Creating a Government That Works Better & Costs Less: Report of the National Performance Review* (Washington: Government Printing Office).

Hagemann, Robert P., and Christoph John, 1995, "The Fiscal Stance in Sweden: A Generational Accounting Perspective," IMF Working Paper 95/105 (Washington: International Monetary Fund).

Haveman, Robert, 1994, "Should Generational Accounts Replace Public Budgets and Deficits?" *Journal of Economic Perspectives*, Vol. 8 (Winter), pp. 95–111.

Heller, Peter S., Richard D. Haas, and Ahsan S. Mansur, 1986, *A Review of the Fiscal Impulse Measure*, IMF Occasional Paper No. 44 (Washington: International Monetary Fund).

Hopkins, Thomas D., 1996, "Regulatory Costs in Profile," Center for the Study of American Business, Policy Study No. 132 (St. Louis, Missouri: Washington University).

Horne, Jocelyn, 1991, "Indicators of Fiscal Sustainability," IMF Working Paper 91/5 (Washington: International Monetary Fund).

International Federation of Accountants, 1995, "Accounting for and Reporting Liabilities," Public Sector Committee Study 6 (New York: IFAC).

———, 1996, *Handbook 1996: Technical Pronouncements* (New York: IFAC).

———, 1997, *Perspectives on Accrual Accounting*, Public Sector Committee, Occasional Paper 3 (New York: IFAC).

International Monetary Fund, 1986, *A Manual on Government Finance Statistics* (Washington).

———, 1995, *Government Finance Statistics Yearbook* (Washington).

———, 1996a, *Government Finance Statistics Manual: Annotated Outline* (Washington).

———, 1996b, *World Economic Outlook, May 1996: A Survey by the Staff of the International Monetary Fund*, World Economic and Financial Surveys (Washington).

———, 1996c, *World Economic Outlook, October 1996: A Survey by the Staff of the International Monetary Fund*, World Economic and Financial Surveys (Washington).

———, and others, 1991, *A Study of the Soviet Economy*, Vol. 1 (Washington: IMF).

Inter-Secretariat Working Group on National Accounts, 1993, *System of National Accounts 1993* (Brussels: Commission of the European Communities).

King, Mervyn A., and Don Fullerton, eds., 1984, *The Taxation of Income from Capital: A Comparative Study in the United States, the United Kingdom, Sweden, and West Germany* (Chicago: University of Chicago Press).

Koedijk, Kees, and Jeroen Kremers, 1996, "Market Opening, Regulation and Growth in Europe," *Economic Policy: A European Forum*, No. 23 (October), pp. 445–85.

Kopits, George, 1991, "Fiscal Reform in European Economies in Transition," in *The Transition to a Market Economy*, Vol. 2, ed. by Salvatore Zecchini and Paul Marer (Paris: Organization for Economic Cooperation and Development), pp. 359–88.

Kotlikoff, Laurence J., 1989, "From Deficit Delusion to the Fiscal Balance Rule: Looking for an Economically Meaningful Way to Assess Fiscal Policy," IMF Working Paper 89/50 (Washington: International Monetary Fund).

Kyrouz, M.E., 1975, "Foreign Tax Rates and Tax Bases," *National Tax Journal*, Vol. 28 (March), pp. 61–80.

Mackenzie, G.A., and Peter Stella, 1996, *Quasi-Fiscal Operations of Public Financial Institutions*, IMF Occasional Paper No. 142 (Washington: International Monetary Fund).

Montanjees, Marie, 1995, "Government Finance Statistics in the Countries of the Former Soviet Union: Compilation and Methodological Issues," IMF Working Paper 95/2 (Washington: International Monetary Fund).

Morin, François, and Claude Dupuy, 1993, *Le Coeur Financier Européen* (Paris: Economica).

New Zealand Treasury, 1996, *Financial Statements of the Government of New Zealand for the Year Ended 30 June 1996* (Wellington).

Okamura, Kenji, 1996, "Japan's Medium- and Long-Term Fiscal Challenges," IMF Working Paper 96/113 (Washington: International Monetary Fund).

Organization for Economic Cooperation and Development, 1990, *Taxpayers' Rights and Obligations: A Survey of the Legal Situation in OECD Countries* (Paris: OECD).

———, 1992, *Regulatory Reform, Privatisation and Competition Policy* (Paris: OECD).

———, 1995a, *Budgeting for Results: Perspectives on Public Expenditure Management* (Paris: OECD).

———, 1995b, *OECD Economic Outlook*, No. 57 (Paris: OECD).

———, 1996a, *Ageing in OECD Countries: A Critical Policy Challenge* (Paris: OECD).

———, 1996b, *National Accounts: Detailed Tables, 1982–94*, Vol. 2 (Paris: OECD).

———, 1996c, *Tax Expenditures: Recent Experiences* (Paris: OECD).

Parker, Karen Elizabeth, and Steffen Kastner, 1993, "A Framework for Assessing Fiscal Sustainability and External Viability, with an Application to India," IMF Working Paper 93/78 (Washington: International Monetary Fund).

Pope, Jeremy, ed., 1996, *National Integrity Systems: The TI Source Book* (Berlin: Transparency International).

Potter, Barry H., 1997, "Dedicated Road Funds—A Preliminary View on a World Bank Initiative," IMF Paper on Policy Analysis and Assessment 97/7 (Washington: International Monetary Fund).

Premchand, A., 1994, "Changing Patterns in Public Expenditure Management: An Overview," IMF Working Paper 94/28 (Washington: International Monetary Fund).

———, 1996, "Erosion of Expenditure Management Systems: An Unintended Consequence of Donor Approaches," IMF Working Paper 96/102 (Washington: International Monetary Fund).

Puviani, Amilcare, 1903, *Teoria della Illusione Finanziaria* (Palermo: Laterza); reprinted as Puviani, Amilcare, and Franco Volpi, 1973, "Teoria della Illusione Finanziaria," *Classici dell'economia politica 13* (Milan: ISEDI).

Reese, Thomas J., 1979, "The Politics of Tax Reform," *National Tax Journal*, Vol. 32 (September), pp. 248–54.

Roseveare, Deborah, and others, 1996, "Ageing Populations, Pension Systems and Government Budgets: Simulations for 20 OECD Countries," Economics Department Working Paper No. 168 (Paris: Organization for Economic Cooperation and Development).

Scott, Graham C., 1996, *Government Reform in New Zealand*, IMF Occasional Paper No. 140 (Washington: International Monetary Fund).

Social Security and Medicare Boards of Trustees, 1995, "Status of the Social Security and Medicare Programs: A Summary of the 1995 Annual Reports," *Tax Notes*, Vol. 67 (May), pp. 837–43.

Tabellini, Guido, 1987, "Secrecy of Monetary Policy and the Variability of Interest Rates," *Journal of Money, Credit and Banking*, Vol. 19 (November), pp. 425–36.

Tanzi, Vito, 1993, "The Budget Deficit in Transition: A Cautionary Note," *Staff Papers*, International Monetary Fund, Vol. 40 (September), pp. 697–707.

————, 1995, "Government Role and the Efficiency of Policy Instruments," IMF Working Paper 95/100 (Washington: International Monetary Fund).

Teijeiro, Mario, 1996, *La Política Fiscal Durante la Convertibilidad, 1991–95* (Buenos Aires: Centro de Estudios Públicos).

United States, Congressional Budget Office, 1996, *The Economic and Budget Outlook: Fiscal Years 1997–2006* (Washington: Government Printing Office).

United States, Department of the Treasury, 1994, *Consolidated Financial Statements* (Washington: Government Printing Office).

————, 1996, *Treasury Bulletin* (Washington: Government Printing Office).

United States, Office of Management and Budget, 1995, *Analytical Perspectives: Budget of United States Government, Fiscal Year 1996* (Washington: Government Printing Office).

————, 1996, *Analytical Perspectives: Budget of the United States Government, Fiscal Year 1997* (Washington: Government Printing Office).

————, 1997, *Analytical Perspectives: Budget of the United States Government, Fiscal Year 1998* (Washington: Government Printing Office).

United States, President's Commission on Budget Concepts, 1967, *Report of the President's Commission on Budget Concepts* (Washington: Government Printing Office).

Van den Noord, Paul, and Richard Herd, 1995, "Estimating Pension Liabilities: A Methodological Framework," OECD Economic Studies, No. 23 (Paris: Organization for Economic Cooperation and Development, February).

von Hagen, Jürgen, and Ian Harden, 1994, "National Budget Processes and Fiscal Performance," in *European Economy: Towards Greater Fiscal Discipline,* Reports and Studies, No. 3 (Brussels: European Commission, Directorate-General for Economic and Financial Affairs).

————, 1996, "Budget Processes and Commitment to Fiscal Discipline," IMF Working Paper 96/78 (Washington: International Monetary Fund).

Wagner, Richard E., 1976, "Revenue Structure, Fiscal Illusion, and Budgetary Choice," *Public Choice*, Vol. 25 (Spring), pp. 45–61.

World Bank, 1994, *Governance: The World Bank's Experience* (Washington).

Recent Occasional Papers of the International Monetary Fund

158. Transparency in Government Operations, by George Kopits and Jon Craig. 1998.

157. Central Bank Reforms in the Baltics, Russia, and the Other Countries of the Former Soviet Union, by a Staff Team led by Malcolm Knight and comprising Susana Almuiña, John Dalton, Inci Otker, Ceyla Pazarbaşıoğlu, Arne B. Petersen, Peter Quirk, Nicholas M. Roberts, Gabriel Sensenbrenner, and Jan Willem van der Vossen. 1997.

156. The ESAF at Ten Years: Economic Adjustment and Reform in Low-Income Countries, by the Staff of the International Monetary Fund. 1997.

155. Fiscal Policy Issues During the Transition in Russia, by Augusto Lopez-Claros and Sergei Alexashenko. 1998.

154. Credibility Without Rules? Monetary Frameworks in the Post–Bretton Woods Era, by Carlo Cottarelli and Curzio Giannini. 1997.

153. Pension Regimes and Saving, by G.A. Mackenzie, Philip Gerson, and Alfredo Cuevas. 1997.

152. Hong Kong, China: Growth, Structural Change, and Economic Stability During the Transition, by John Dodsworth and Dubravko Mihaljek. 1997.

151. Currency Board Arrangements: Issues and Experiences, by a staff team led by Tomás J.T. Baliño and Charles Enoch. 1997.

150. Kuwait: From Reconstruction to Accumulation for Future Generations, by Nigel Andrew Chalk, Mohamed A. El-Erian, Susan J. Fennell, Alexei P. Kireyev, and John F. Wison. 1997.

149. The Composition of Fiscal Adjustment and Growth: Lessons from Fiscal Reforms in Eight Economies, by G.A. Mackenzie, David W.H. Orsmond, and Philip R. Gerson. 1997.

148. Nigeria: Experience with Structural Adjustment, by Gary Moser, Scott Rogers, and Reinold van Til, with Robin Kibuka and Inutu Lukonga. 1997.

147. Aging Populations and Public Pension Schemes, by Sheetal K. Chand and Albert Jaeger. 1996.

146. Thailand: The Road to Sustained Growth, by Kalpana Kochhar, Louis Dicks-Mireaux, Balazs Horvath, Mauro Mecagni, Erik Offerdal, and Jianping Zhou. 1996.

145. Exchange Rate Movements and Their Impact on Trade and Investment in the APEC Region, by Takatoshi Ito, Peter Isard, Steven Symansky, and Tamim Bayoumi. 1996.

144. National Bank of Poland: The Road to Indirect Instruments, by Piero Ugolini. 1996.

143. Adjustment for Growth: The African Experience, by Michael T. Hadjimichael, Michael Nowak, Robert Sharer, and Amor Tahari. 1996.

142. Quasi-Fiscal Operations of Public Financial Institutions, by G.A. Mackenzie and Peter Stella. 1996.

141. Monetary and Exchange System Reforms in China: An Experiment in Gradualism, by Hassanali Mehran, Marc Quintyn, Tom Nordman, and Bernard Laurens. 1996.

140. Government Reform in New Zealand, by Graham C. Scott. 1996.

139. Reinvigorating Growth in Developing Countries: Lessons from Adjustment Policies in Eight Economies, by David Goldsbrough, Sharmini Coorey, Louis Dicks-Mireaux, Balazs Horvath, Kalpana Kochhar, Mauro Mecagni, Erik Offerdal, and Jianping Zhou. 1996.

138. Aftermath of the CFA Franc Devaluation, by Jean A.P. Clément, with Johannes Mueller, Stéphane Cossé, and Jean Le Dem. 1996.

137. The Lao People's Democratic Republic: Systemic Transformation and Adjustment, edited by Ichiro Otani and Chi Do Pham. 1996.

136. Jordan: Strategy for Adjustment and Growth, edited by Edouard Maciejewski and Ahsan Mansur. 1996.

135. Vietnam: Transition to a Market Economy, by John R. Dodsworth, Erich Spitäller, Michael Braulke, Keon Hyok Lee, Kenneth Miranda, Christian Mulder, Hisanobu Shishido, and Krishna Srinivasan. 1996.

134. India: Economic Reform and Growth, by Ajai Chopra, Charles Collyns, Richard Hemming, and Karen Parker with Woosik Chu and Oliver Fratzscher. 1995.

133. Policy Experiences and Issues in the Baltics, Russia, and Other Countries of the Former Soviet Union, edited by Daniel A. Citrin and Ashok K. Lahiri. 1995.

132. Financial Fragilities in Latin America: The 1980s and 1990s, by Liliana Rojas-Suárez and Steven R. Weisbrod. 1995.

131. Capital Account Convertibility: Review of Experience and Implications for IMF Policies, by staff teams headed by Peter J. Quirk and Owen Evans. 1995.

130. Challenges to the Swedish Welfare State, by Desmond Lachman, Adam Bennett, John H. Green, Robert Hagemann, and Ramana Ramaswamy. 1995.

129. IMF Conditionality: Experience Under Stand-By and Extended Arrangements. Part II: Background Papers. Susan Schadler, Editor, with Adam Bennett, Maria Carkovic, Louis Dicks-Mireaux, Mauro Mecagni, James H.J. Morsink, and Miguel A. Savastano. 1995.

128. IMF Conditionality: Experience Under Stand-By and Extended Arrangements. Part I: Key Issues and Findings, by Susan Schadler, Adam Bennett, Maria Carkovic, Louis Dicks-Mireaux, Mauro Mecagni, James H.J. Morsink, and Miguel A. Savastano. 1995.

127. Road Maps of the Transition: The Baltics, the Czech Republic, Hungary, and Russia, by Biswajit Banerjee, Vincent Koen, Thomas Krueger, Mark S. Lutz, Michael Marrese, and Tapio O. Saavalainen. 1995.

126. The Adoption of Indirect Instruments of Monetary Policy, by a staff team headed by William E. Alexander, Tomás J.T. Baliño, and Charles Enoch. 1995.

125. United Germany: The First Five Years—Performance and Policy Issues, by Robert Corker, Robert A. Feldman, Karl Habermeier, Hari Vittas, and Tessa van der Willigen. 1995.

124. Saving Behavior and the Asset Price "Bubble" in Japan: Analytical Studies, edited by Ulrich Baumgartner and Guy Meredith. 1995.

123. Comprehensive Tax Reform: The Colombian Experience, edited by Parthasarathi Shome. 1995.

122. Capital Flows in the APEC Region, edited by Mohsin S. Khan and Carmen M. Reinhart. 1995.

121. Uganda: Adjustment with Growth, 1987–94, by Robert L. Sharer, Hema R. De Zoysa, and Calvin A. McDonald. 1995.

120. Economic Dislocation and Recovery in Lebanon, by Sena Eken, Paul Cashin, S. Nuri Erbas, Jose Martelino, and Adnan Mazarei. 1995.

119. Singapore: A Case Study in Rapid Development, edited by Kenneth Bercuson with a staff team comprising Robert G. Carling, Aasim M. Husain, Thomas Rumbaugh, and Rachel van Elkan. 1995.

118. Sub-Saharan Africa: Growth, Savings, and Investment, by Michael T. Hadjimichael, Dhaneshwar Ghura, Martin Mühleisen, Roger Nord, and E. Murat Uçer. 1995.

117. Resilience and Growth Through Sustained Adjustment: The Moroccan Experience, by Saleh M. Nsouli, Sena Eken, Klaus Enders, Van-Can Thai, Jörg Decressin, and Filippo Cartiglia, with Janet Bungay. 1995.

116. Improving the International Monetary System: Constraints and Possibilities, by Michael Mussa, Morris Goldstein, Peter B. Clark, Donald J. Mathieson, and Tamim Bayoumi. 1994.

115. Exchange Rates and Economic Fundamentals: A Framework for Analysis, by Peter B. Clark, Leonardo Bartolini, Tamim Bayoumi, and Steven Symansky. 1994.

114. Economic Reform in China: A New Phase, by Wanda Tseng, Hoe Ee Khor, Kalpana Kochhar, Dubravko Mihaljek, and David Burton. 1994.

113. Poland: The Path to a Market Economy, by Liam P. Ebrill, Ajai Chopra, Charalambos Christofides, Paul Mylonas, Inci Otker, and Gerd Schwartz. 1994.

112. The Behavior of Non-Oil Commodity Prices, by Eduardo Borensztein, Mohsin S. Khan, Carmen M. Reinhart, and Peter Wickham. 1994.

111. The Russian Federation in Transition: External Developments, by Benedicte Vibe Christensen. 1994.

110. Limiting Central Bank Credit to the Government: Theory and Practice, by Carlo Cottarelli. 1993.

109. The Path to Convertibility and Growth: The Tunisian Experience, by Saleh M. Nsouli, Sena Eken, Paul Duran, Gerwin Bell, and Zühtü Yücelik. 1993.

108. Recent Experiences with Surges in Capital Inflows, by Susan Schadler, Maria Carkovic, Adam Bennett, and Robert Kahn. 1993.

107. China at the Threshold of a Market Economy, by Michael W. Bell, Hoe Ee Khor, and Kalpana Kochhar with Jun Ma, Simon N'guiamba, and Rajiv Lall. 1993.

Note: For information on the title and availability of Occasional Papers not listed, please consult the IMF Publications Catalog or contact IMF Publication Services.